CONTEMPORARY POLITICAL PROTEST

Contemporary Political Protest

Essays on political militancy

ABBY PETERSON
Göteborg University, Sweden

Ashgate

Aldershot • Burlington USA • Singapore • Sydney

Published by
Ashgate Publishing Limited
Gower House
Croft Road
Aldershot
Hampshire GU11 3HR
England

Ashgate Publishing Company
131 Main Street
Burlington, VT 05401-5600 USA

Ashgate website: http://www.ashgate.com

British Library Cataloguing in Publication Data
Peterson, Abby
    Contemporary political protest : essays on political
    militancy
    1.Political violence - History - 20th Century 2.Protest
    movements - History - 20th Century
    I.Title
    303.6

Library of Congress Control Number: 2001091688

ISBN 0 7546 0569 8

Printed in Great Britain by
Antony Rowe Ltd, Chippenham, Wiltshire

[issu)

Contents

Introduction

A new type of political violence among young people has begun to gain momentum throughout Europe. We are witnessing a wave of militant political actions, which has even entered the Swedish alternative political culture. For example, young racist and antiracist activists are confronting each other (and often the police riot squads) on the streets of Sweden, and the 'spectacles' of the confrontations are welding them together in respective groups. (Peterson, 1995 and 1997) Neo-fascist youth groups have carried out arson attacks against refugee centres throughout Sweden; neo-nazi youth have also claimed responsibility for the murders of a number of immigrant youth as well as homosexuals. Young environmental and animal right's activists are increasingly using violent means to convey their moral outrage over companies, which they regard as a danger to the environment and animals. For example, in Sweden, militant vegetarian and 'vegan' youth have burned down hotdog stands and refrigeration trucks, and have carried out arson attacks on meatpacking firms and retailers. Militant 'green youth' are organising for struggle against the construction of the Öresund Bridge and the 'Dennis package' in Stockholm. A group of young people from Örebro demonstrated their dissatisfaction with the European Union referendum and 'shot' police with slingshots from an occupied building. These are examples of militant youth groups with a political message, both from the 'far left' and the 'far right'.

The 'supremacy of praxis', a doctrine of the primacy of direct militant action developed by Andreas Baader and Ulrike Meinhof, *Rote Armé* activists in the early 1970s, finds resonance in a new militant political culture emerging in Sweden. Baader and Meinhof argued that their 'cause' could not be expressed in words, rather it was constituted through their actions. *RAF* grounded its action doctrine in a notion borrowed from Italian theorist and activist Antonio Gramsci — *conditio sine qua non* — the strong will as the motor in the revolutionary process whereby subjectivity becomes praxis. In this *RAF* interpretation of Gramsci, it appears to have been the 'strong will' of Andreas Baader, which functioned as the motor in the revolutionary process. Contemporary militant activists have more or less left this reliance upon the force of an individual charismatic leader(s) as the initiator of the revolutionary process, preferring to lay focus upon the process itself, which constructs and stark enhances the meaning of the militant Group ('subjectivity becomes praxis'). Nevertheless, aside from the force of individual personalities emphasised by their historical antecedents in *RAF*, the underlying notion of actions defining the group lies at the basis for even today's militant groups. Militant activists today are putting 'deeds before words' and are claiming that "it always pays to resist". And resisting they are, employing increasingly violent enactments in order to extend their political messages to the polity. In this book we will investigate this new wave of militancy which has infiltrated even the historically 'non-violent' alternative political culture which once dominated in Sweden.

Firstly, militancy is defined throughout this book with an extended notion of violence. Militant action groups/action networks stage enactments of violence — self-directed, other-directed, and/or property directed — which are anticipated, threatened or actual. With this extended notion of violent enactments which includes often expressly Gandhian principles of 'non-violence', for example militant activists putting their 'lives on the line' for their cause or militant groups symbolically 'disarming' the nose-cone of a fighter jet, we are better able to capture the breadth of this new wave of political militancy emerging. Particularly left-wing militants in Sweden have tended to shy away from other-directed enactments of violence, preferring tactics which are directed against property, and increasingly, to innovative tactics which are self-directed violent enactments. These violent enactments broadcast to the polity the bodily self-determination and commitment to their struggle on the part of these activists. More and more it is what the activists *do* which makes them militant and their politics radical, not what they *say*.

Secondly, while more traditional social movement factions and networks depend upon their effectiveness on the mobilisation of action that require participants to *stop* everyday routines and *step outside* of their everyday lives, militant action groups/action networks exercise their power more fundamentally by fostering historical action emotionally and corporeally *within the framework of everyday roles and relationships*. (Cf. Flacks, 1988) The militant social movement activists we are focussing upon in this book intimately integrate their political practices of protest within the framework of their everyday roles and relationships — "protest is my whole life", as Laura, a 16 year-old Swedish Animal Liberation Front activist, expressed her political engagement and commitment for animals.

Unlike militant protests that solely lodge claims to entrance into the polity, the moral and emotional militant resistance communities articulate their political beliefs within everyday life and hence are semi-private performances of their political identity(ies). The overtly political performances of militant activists are, nevertheless, inseparable from the processes of articulation of the militant resistance community in sites of collective identity construction submerged within everyday life. Militant political protest acquires its force, its creativity, its subversiveness, and its credibility, through its sub-political articulation in everyday life. The militant 'practices what he/she preaches'.

Whether these militant resistance communities are a retreat from the public arena, which is the arena or agora of politics, behind the surfaces of individual activists entrenched within the sub-political arena of everyday life, or is an element in their collective political action which ultimately must open to the political space of public deliberation is an empirical question which must be posed to every action network which relies upon 'personal' corporeal and emotional statements of moralised political behaviour. These militant resistance communities may indeed remain sub-political, that is, remain as collective identities, which do not lodge claims to be heard in the polity. However, overt militant political protest must rest (to a certain degree) upon their 'sub-political' articulation.

The Research

The research for this book was carried out primarily by Lillemor Thyberg during the period 1996-1999 with extensive field work, which included collecting 39 interviews with left-wing militant activists across the range of militant action groups/action networks in Sweden active during this period. Furthermore, field observations were carried out of a variety of militant actions: an occupation and several militant confrontations between young antiracists and racist networks. And lastly, we monitored the alternative media developed by these groups, their newspapers and newsletters, and most importantly, their Internet chat sites. When this project was initially formulated we could not anticipate the extent to which Internet would prove to be a valuable empirical source in our research. Literally, during a few short years, the Internet became the prime media for communication among militant groups/action networks, together with their face-to-face channels of communication. Thousands of pages were generated each month within these militant action networks where strategies and goals were the subjects of ongoing debate among sympathisers and opponents alike. By tapping into these sites an enormous, and relatively 'open', militant discourse was made available to us. Our face-to-face interviews proved to be a complement and 'check' upon these 'virtual' sources.

Our access to certain restricted circuits of militant discourse and culture depended upon our recognition of the thresholds of secrecy. This recognition had to be visibly displayed by us in our dialogues and in our interactions with militant activists — in our face-to-face interactions as well as in our 'virtual' interactions on, and monitoring of, Internet sites. Our meetings with informants were transactions on the political borders of Swedish society — which were inevitably restricted exchanges of information. In the field, in order to maintain our credibility with our informants, as well as protect their identities and certain 'strategic' secrets of their groups, a sort of 'mutual editing' took place. In the field this was a co-construction of silence and speech, where silence was recognised and validated. (Cf. Feldman, 1991: chapter one.)

In the analysis phase of the research this co-construction of speech and silence, while it was respected to a degree, i.e. anonymity of the informants is maintained, it was also transgressed. This is an unavoidable schism inherent between the phases of data collection and data analysis that in research of this type poses ethical dilemmas for the researchers. While secrecy could be respected and maintained as to certain elements in our empirical materials, secrecy was nevertheless analysed and problematised. At this stage in our research process we allowed ourselves to take a step back from this co-construction of silence and speech which was essential in the field and re-enter a critical 'gaze' — analysing both 'speech' and 'silence' in order to understand the gap between what was 'said' — speech — and what was 'not said' — silence. Gaps were also identified in 'speech' among the militant groups/action networks we were investigating where we penetrated into the often-mystifying argot of these groups. Furthermore, in our analysis we were confronting the disparity between words and acts, attempting to lay bare this inevitable gap in political action. It is a provisional analysis of these three gaps — 1) the blank spaces between speech and silence; 2) the blank spaces within speech; and, 3) the blank spaces between speech and acts; — which are the analytical focal points throughout this book. This analysis of blank spaces, its recognition and subsequent problematisation of secrecy, embraces at best, I hope, *experiments* with the reality of militant action I have observed and reported here.

Outline of the Book

This book includes five essays which all deal with various aspects of political militancy, 'experiments', if you like, in attempts to grasp the new forms of political militancy emerging today. In chapter one I touch upon two recurring theoretical themes in the book, that of the grounding of militant political action in time and place which recognises the 'real' geographies of militant action; and, which emphasises that these 'real' geographies would be unnavigitable without cognitive 'maps of meaning'. Militant groups/action networks construct action spaces: territorial, temporal, and cognitive. Furthermore, these action spaces, whether they are territorial, temporal or cognitive, are both unstable and penetrable. They are all subject to the hijacking efforts of rival militant groups/action networks, as are their boundaries penetrable to both the police as well as sympathisers, they are inextricably linked to social relations and practices beyond their 'boundaries'.

Young people are pushed to the margins of power within society — prohibited from speaking as moral and political agents. They are restricted from speaking in those spheres where public deliberation shapes social policy and refused the power to make knowledge consequential with respect to their own individual and collective needs. (Cf. Giroux, 1998) Nevertheless, despite these restrictions of public speech, speak they do. While of course there are exceptions, the vast majority of militant activists in Sweden are young people struggling, so to say, to enter polity through self-constructed 'backdoors' or 'tunnelling in' from sites below these spheres for public deliberation to which they are denied entry. Militant resistance in general is most often trivialised in that it is associated with 'coming-of-age' rebellion, deemed as a sign of youthful immaturity for the role of responsible citizenship. Further in chapter one we will investigate a specific case of young people's attempt to define their own role as responsible citizens, to make their voices heard in what they perceive as a deaf polity. An occupation of an abandoned brewery in a small community in western Sweden is analysed in terms of the construction and reconstruction of the action spaces of militancy.

While the role of emotions in the political processes of social movements has not been entirely neglected by sociologists — both earlier and contemporary — it has nevertheless all too often been relegated to a 'supporting role' in the drama of politics. In chapter two I will engage with the role of emotions in militant actions, that actions 'speak louder than words' because of the emotive force they leash and unleash. In earlier work I have sought to examine how ritual confrontations have generated emotional states which are a fundamental basis for the collective identity construction among militant political groups/action networks. Their collective identity construction, their emotional sense of community or 'we', rather than being a motive for social movement participation, is both the precondition for collective militant action *and* the result of their collective militant actions.

It is in this context that I have discussed what I termed *neo-sectarianism* — phenomena not new or unique to contemporary societies approaching the *fin du millennium*, but one that even preoccupied the social critics and analysts of modernity at the *fin de siécle*. (Peterson, 1995 and 1997) In this work I analysed the collective identity construction of militant groups, what I designate there as neo-sects, on the basis of three fundamental mechanisms for group 'fusion': ideology, cultural praxis, and confrontation. I placed emphasis upon the interactive processes of conflict, i.e. ritual confrontation, which fosters a mentality of embattlement creating a vision of the world as divided between 'we' and 'them'. I argue that this mentality of embattlement is particularly enhanced by their lived experiences of physical confrontations with their adversaries, be these confrontations with the police, military, or other youth groups. Radicalisation and group fusion follow the everyday emotional and physical experiences of conflict and turmoil on the part of militants in their action spaces.

After looking at the phenomenon we are theorising in terms of the emotive force of confrontation — political militancy in contemporary Sweden — in focus in the remaining pages of the chapter is the work of Émile Durkheim for an understanding of the contemporary forms of militant political 'groupism', *sic* neo-sectarianism, emerging.

Chapter three deals with the visible, passionate bodies of militant political resistance — the ways in which the body 'embodies' political struggle, i.e. the ways in which the body is implicated in militant political resistance and the ways political messages are 'bodied forth'. In the struggle against existing structures of power the body is the most primary interface of powers of resistance. However, the body is more than an interface of the powers of resistance, the militant body *is* a power of resistance. Through enactments of violence — self-directed, other-directed and/or property-directed — which are anticipated, threatened or actual, the militant body is constructed as a formation of political agency.   In the sense of body discussed by Eugene Halton (1995) as an ability to "body forth" meaning, the militant body bodies forth political meaning. Feelings, emotions, lived and living experiences of oppression and resistance, even bodily secretions such as adrenaline and sweat, are brought directly to bear upon a political struggle. Theirs is the 'hot' struggle of passions, far removed from the tepid bodies and deliberating 'Cartesian heads' of institutional politics. This is not to say, however, that the militant body is headless or mindless, rather, the rationality of militant actions simply more directly and patently rests upon bodily lived/living experiences — the body is implicated in a more immediate sense to the rationality of militant action, which while rational, is not necessarily 'reasonable' action.

Neglected in my earlier analyses was the role secrecy plays for the collective identity construction of neo-sects, the 'groupism' inherent in militant political cultures. In chapter four I focus upon the role of secrecy in radical political struggle. The analysis builds upon the work of Georg Simmel, who more than any other social theorist has conceptualised the secret society as a specific form of sociality. Rather than attempting to define secrecy, or the group which is fundamentally bonded through the communicative acts of secrecy, so-called secret societies, I seek to explicate its essential features by examining the forms it takes which connects to Simmels' original characterisation of secrecy as a form that is invariant to content. Furthermore, in focusing upon the forms secret societies, *sic* neo-sects, assume, underlines the continuum which secrecy, as a bonding principle, plays in specific militant political groups within specific socio-political contexts. In other words, while political high-risk militancy requires to some degree secrecy, it is always a question of more or less, and subsequently, secrecy is more or less an underlying principle in their collective bonding, i.e. in their construction of collective identity. It is argued that the protection of secrecy is the rational organisation of emotions. The foundation of secrecy both confirms and reinforces the basic solidarity — the be-ing together — upon which the secret society, *sic* neo-sect, rests.

Media modernity is a precondition for the contemporary politics of militancy and opens opportunities for militant groups to spread their messages — their symbolic challenges and meaning contestation — beyond the locales of their immediate actions. Not only is the media space opened a precondition for the politics of militancy, but also it seems that in the post-modern world, the media are rapidly becoming the sites of politics itself. In chapter five I look at the friend and/or foe relations militant political groups/action networks have with the channels of media modernity.

Further, in this concluding chapter I look more closely at alternative media channels, which have become increasingly both the means and the sites for militant political action. The politics of militancy has more and more moved its terrain of political action to the relatively uncharted virtual territory opened up by Internet. The 1990s have witnessed the advent of a new militant politics in cyberspatial political terrain; 'cyberwars' — anticipated, threatened or actual — are being fought on Internet. The application of new alternative media — tactical media — to militant political action goes beyond established media channels and exists well outside of the realm of parliamentarian or electoral forms of politics. These are media applications that both include and move beyond the discursive and dialogic model of democracy, adding the dimension and confrontational style of direct militant action.

Acknowledgements

In researching these topics and writing this book, many people have contributed to my work. First and foremost, I thank Lillemor Thyberg for her insightful and sensitive fieldwork, as well as those activists who have allowed us to interview them, generously sharing their experiences of militant political action with inquisitive researchers. I am deeply indebted to a number of scholars who have read and provided thoughtful comments on parts of the manuscript: Zygmunt Bauman, Sandro Fridlizius, Jeffrey C. Goldfarb, Kyra Landzelius, Alberto Melucci, Birgitta Nedelmann, Carlo Ruzza, Lisbeth Stenberg, and Lillemor Thyberg. On a more personal note, I wish to extend a particular thank-you to Zygmunt Bauman and Alberto Melucci, who have both been enormous sources of intellectual inspiration over the years, and who have offered me the personal support and friendship necessary for my own intellectual pursuits along the often lonely and crooked path of 'theorising' political action. Lisbeth Stenberg has provided the emotional day-to-day support I needed to finish this project, even during the most difficult of times, for which I extend a heart-felt thank-you.

The research was supported financially through a generous three-year grant from 'The Bank of Sweden Tercentenary Foundation'. Finally, I wish to thank all of my colleagues at the Department of Sociology, Göteborg University, who together make up the intellectual context I call 'home'.

1 The Action Spaces of Militancy

In this chapter the action spaces of militant groups/action networks will be understood heuristically on two distinct, while intimately interrelated, analytical levels: the *temporal action space* and the *territorial action space* which both recognise and emphasise the 'real' geographies of militant action. However, these 'real' geographies of militant action are nevertheless cognitively informed in order to acquire meaning, without "maps of meaning" these 'real' geographies of militant action would be unnavigitable, their social relations unintelligible. (Cf. Clarke et al., 1976:10) While the 'real' geographies of militant social action are recurrent themes in the book and will be more explicitly extricated here, the underlying thread throughout this book is the ongoing constructions and reconstructions of militant collective identities. Collective identity for Alberto Melucci (1995 and 1989) is the process of constructing an action system, i.e. an interactive and shared definition produced by a number of individuals and/or groups concerning the orientations of their action and the field of opportunities and constraints in which such action is to take place. Put in slightly different terms, collective identity is the construction of an action space — a cognitive understanding concerning the ends, means and field of action which is negotiated and renegotiated through a recurrent process of activation of the relations that bind actors together. So if this is the overarching action space — the *cognitive action space* — it is nevertheless bounded in time and place and is inextricably interwoven in the temporal and territorial action spaces.

While the notion of space is ambiguous, the notion of action in contemporary militant wings of social movements is emphasised. Ulrike Meinhof talked of the 'supremacy of praxis' and what I have designated as a political neo-sect tends to have a clear-cut strategy that valorises action, rather than 'talk'. As one of my young informants stated: "it always pays to resist". (Peterson, 1997a) Militant groups regard taking action as a fundamental source of empowerment. So, if

1

the notion of spaces of militancy is ambiguous, not so the connectedness between militancy and action. These are spaces where action is taken, where the militant construction of action spaces is caught in the dramatic cross-fire of power and history, political economy and grounded struggle pervading cultural practices situated in any landscape or temporality of militant 'resistance'.

The Temporal Action Space — Events 'Taking' Place

The temporal militant action space understood analytically is time bounded, it is the action space of an *event*, either constructed by the militant activists or a socio-cultural event which is 'reconstructed' by militant social movement action. Militant political actions *take* place. In other words, these events are temporary and hence bounded in time and can either be constructed solely by militant action, e.g. a staged illegal demonstration, an occupation of a building, the bombing of an antagonist's premises, a 'liberation' of laboratory animals — the symbolical construction and manifestation of a cognitive action space within the perimeters of a bounded temporal action space. Or the event may be a 'reconstruction' of another socio-cultural event — a ritual event — in terms of a militant group's/action network's meaning construction, e.g. the counter-demonstrations outside of the Democratic Presidential Convention in Chicago in 1968, and the Black Panther manifestation by Tommie Smith and John Carlos when they raised their clenched fists with black gloves during the American national anthem on the podium at the Mexico City Summer Olympics in 1968 are but two examples of militant groups/action networks 'hijacking' ritual events and the media space opened by them. A militant group/ action network can even hijack the temporal action space constructed through the actions of another militant group/action; i.e. another temporal action space is entered and used by often opposing groups to redefine the event and the media space opened by it. A neo-nazi manifestation often attracts antiracist activists to counter-demonstrations and confrontations, an often-welcome addition to the neo-nazi temporal action space as it elicits media attention. (See Peterson, 1997)

Militant groups and action networks develop temporal practices (most often in conjunction with spatial practices which will be discussed in the following section) which are designed to control or to interrupt the temporal action space of events — to intervene in historicity. Spectacular temporal innovations have been developed by militant eco-protesters in Britain, and these temporal tactics have spread throughout Europe among activists engaged in militant protest. They have successfully used new, effective and imaginative tactics as primarily a means to prolong an occupation of, for example, road development sites, quarries, city streets. The tactical innovations which have emerged within the radical ecology movement in Britain provide us with dramatic examples of militant activists creatively controlling the temporal action space of protest, which if for nothing else is essential for their successful intervention in mass media, thereby capturing the public's attention. Furthermore, the symbolic use of their bodies in the action relay to the public the moral commitment of the activists in their struggle. (See chapter three, this volume)

Less spectacular, but perhaps far more impressive, is the case of 'Action Group Kynnefjället's' temporal strategies. In response to the threat that their mountain, located on the West Coast of southern Sweden, would be the site of nuclear waste disposal, hundreds of activists arrived high on this mountain plateau to stop efforts to begin test drilling. With 'human chains' they stopped the trucks from ascending the mountain. With kites and balloons on strings they stopped the helicopter from landing. With these action innovations their protest was 'temporarily' successful. There was no test drilling in the mountain. This was over 20 years ago. Ever since 1980 activists have held 'guard' over their mountain in a small red cabin, day and night, 365 days a year. This action group is somewhat of a social movement anomaly in Sweden where militant social movement activists are overwhelmingly young people. During their vigil on the mountain fifty activists have died, the average age in their action group is about sixty-five, but over a hundred activists remain, taking their turn on guard in the cabin. Their stubborn struggle has reached the Guinness Record Book, but they are dedicated to persistently struggle on as long as no permanent, and what they consider safe, disposal is found for radioactive waste materials. According to an interview with a 71 year-old retired farmer, "it is nature and our distrust which keeps us going". The 69 year-old woman who is the acting chair of the action group explains that:

We have been handed over this great and beautiful mountain, let us then leave it to coming generations. That is our attitude to life. We maintain a guard for our grandchildren.

The quote above reveals the multiple temporalities implicated in a militant group's actions — their ongoing struggle in the *present* to preserve their mountain, a 'gift' from a primordial *past* for *future* generations. While the temporal action space, the action event, is 'bounded' *in* time, its temporality is ambivalent.

Bhabha (1990) claims that 'the people' within the contested cultural territory of the nation space are in 'double-time'. On the one hand, they are:

"the historical 'objects' of a nationalist pedagogy, giving the discourse an authority that is based on the pregiven or constituted historical origin or event", on the other hand, "the people are also the 'subjects' of a process of signification that must erase any prior or originary presence of the nation-people to demonstrate the prodigious, living principle of the people as that continual process by which the national life is redeemed and signified as a repeating and reproductive process" (p. 297) — the rags and patches of everyday life.

The people as agents are in ambivalent *movement* between pedagogical time and performative time, challenging the narrative authority of history with their actions in the here and now, *in* time. Social movement action is in movement between the past — history — and the present, moving between these temporalities in complicated processes of both challenge and learning, bringing the past to bear in different ways on the present, and even the future. Militant activists may claim the accumulated memory of a particular place as their own in a symbolical struggle to redefine history itself. For example, in Sweden, which lacks much of the temporal anchor of the monumental architecture found on the continent of Europe — sites like the Brandenburg Gate and the Arch de Triumph, storage sites for stories of events — historical reconstruction is often fought on a more symbolic plane than the terrain of place. However, for neo-nazi groups and extreme right-wing groups in general, the statues of King Charles XII, the 16th century 'warrior king', which adorn many of the city squares in Sweden, have become a sought after site for their public actions in their temporal strategies to 'recapture' history; the stored memories of the notion of Sweden that are inscribed in these statues.

Moreover, as militant action is perceived as actions imbued with intent, that is, actions to challenge and change hegemonic relations of power, this action invokes the future as well. Militant action takes place in an 'imaginary' dialogue between past, present and future. Militant action acts *on* time to bring about a possible future circumstance, and as such, this action always has a teleological aspect, however moderate and unpretentious its goals are for acting *in* time. In short, the temporal action space of militant groups/action networks is caught in ambivalent movement in *'triple-time'*, where the rhythms of the past, present and future are brought in an unstable and tentative harmony.

The Territorial Action Space — Places That Matter

The territorial action space of militancy understood analytically is geographically bounded; it is the action space of *place* or territory. Militant activists act through specific geographies: e.g. on the streets, outside of military bases, surrounding a historical monument, an abandoned building; around specific geographical entities such as the nation, 'our turf', a mountain, or Third World rainforests; or, over other kinds of geographies or 'places' such as jamming government web sites in cyberspace. These are all examples of what Pile (1997) has called "geographies of resistance". The territorial action space is not a preconstructed and fully formed stage upon which militant actions are played out, rather territorial action spaces — the places of militant social action — are both constructed or 'created' by militant actions and are at the same time co-constitutive of these same militant actions. Militant groups/action networks make use of extent geographies and make 'new' geographies, just as geographies make militant action.

A territorial action space, within its boundaries militant activists take *place*, is just as cognitively defined, hence ambiguous, as the temporal action space. Militant action does not only take place in place; it also seeks to appropriate space, to make new spaces of places. Tightly interwoven in militant social actions in territorial place are the ongoing mappings and re-mappings of the space of place. Maps keep track of territories, but territories never quite reveal themselves on any map. The territory generates conflicts and identities rooted in particular places. And it is here, beneath the flight path of media flows and beneath the attempts by militant groups to capture territory on a map, that, according to McKenzie Wark (1994), "the genealogy of struggle remains". (p. 63) (Cf. Wray 1998b) Subsequently, even if cognitive processes of mapping generate forms of collective action, these cognitive maps, caught in the information flows of media vectors, are quite different from the territorial action spaces.

The 'place' of militant social action is embedded in multiple layers of meanings; subsequently, the territorial action space of a militant group/action network is embedded in different scales that mutually influence each other. Hence militant action can be found inscribed on the surface of the body, 'contained' within a specific 'place' in a local setting, and in turn located within a specific national territory in a global universe. And while scale is an important consideration for the analysis of social actions in general, the scale of social spaces are not, as Doreen Massey argues (1998), tidily organised in distinct scales, e.g. body, home, community, nation, global, but as complicated nets of interrelations in which militant actions are differently located. Firstly, the territorial action space of militancy is hence a vast complexity of interconnections, which places firm emphasis upon the *links* or *openings* between the 'real geographies' of social action. Massey argues that the social relations that constitute geographical space are not organised into scales so much as:

> into *constellations of temporary coherence* ... set within a social space which is the product of relations and interconnections from the very local to the intercontinental. (pp. 124-125)

Secondly, while militant groups/action networks act in geographical places, struggling to appropriate place in conjunction with its cognitive action space, its map of place, where the sense of place is articulated on two planes — map and territory — it is crucial for an understanding of militant action that they are elements engaged in a struggle against forces of domination. Partly, militant groups/action networks act on topographies imposed through the spatial technologies of domination, and partly their actions move across the topographies of domination "under the noses of the enemy, seeking to create new meanings out of imposed meanings, to re-work and divert space to other ends". (Pile, 1997:16)

Consequently, the actions of militant groups/action networks take place in the places controlled by practices of domination, but nevertheless subvert these places and hence these practices, moving across them in efforts to re-spatialise them, lend them new meanings. Their 'room' to manoeuvre in a struggle against authorities which superimposes itself onto physical places is across and beneath these places, in the inevitable cracks which exist and which involve alternative spaces which are dimly lit, deliberately hidden, and saturated with memories. And while the actions of militant groups/ action networks subvert practices of domination, their actions cannot be separated from practices of domination, they are "hybrid practices", which always bear some trace of the practices of domination. (Routledge, 1997: 70) An example are the suppression of internal heterogeneity and practices of domination within specific militant groups in order to further the 'wider cause' of the action network or social movement which are themselves a reproduction of dominating power structures.

Thirdly, the actions of militants take place through, across, beneath and 'in' places involving the spatialities of location and boundary formation and maintenance, however, their actions are also constituted through the notion of movement. That is, the actions of militant groups/action networks are understood spatially as *movement* in time and it is this sense of movement, a change from one 'place' in the topography of power to another, from one 'place' on the cognitive map of its social relations to another, which underlies its transformative power. This movement, however, does not necessarily originate from one single place nor does it necessarily follow one single path over an overt political terrain, rather it is often constituted of tiny micro-movements of resistance from a number of points and travels often on many paths towards many destinations with many aims. (Cf. Deleuze and Guattari, 1987) We can at best momentarily discern ephemeral constellations of actions by militant groups that only allude to an imagined unity in the struggle.

Within the complexity of the militant group interaction within territorial space, militant groups/action networks are constantly engaged in efforts to *territorialise*, to claim spaces, to include some and exclude others from particular 'places'. Efforts to fence off places may be part of militant network tactics to protect and defend particular groups and interests. And as Massey (1998) points out, fencing off a place may also be an expression of attempts to dominate, and to control and define others. However, both inclusion and exclusion tactics underlining spatial organisation — territorialisation processes — are fundamentally bound up with the social construction of identities. Perhaps the nation-state most readily comes to mind as an example of a project of territorialisation; a configuration of social relations constructing the social space we have come during the last 200 years to designate as the nation-state — a particular area excluded for some, including others, a sovereign territory in some respects, its sovereignty challenged in other respects. (Peterson, 1996a) While the nation-state may very well, and most often does, have regulated, guarded physical boundaries, these boundaries are not impermeable to the global flows of goods, capital, people, cultural products and information. Even the most 'closed' nation-states, those which most rigorously lay claims to a particular geographic place and most rigorously patrol its boundaries, will have its inevitable 'doors' to without, its boundaries superseded and transgressed, reminding us of the interconnectedness of any geographical place, and the subsequent interconnectedness of the spatiality of place.

On a smaller scale we have the case of territorialisation processes by protest movements at roadsites. Docherty (1997) argues that protests at road sites are a form of siege warfare.

> Protesters occupy a site and build defences. The defences are in trees, houses, or underground tunnels. ... Aside from the considerable amount of work invested in building site defences, there are also forays into enemy territory. Contractors' offices are occupied, and shareholders' meeting are disrupted. (p. 5)

Here we find both tactics of territorialisation and deterritorialisation: territorialising by holding and defending a geographical place, not through a defence or place occupation on the basis of the sheer numbers of activists assembled, but through the use of technical innovations through which a small number of committed activists can successfully defend place for a more or less extended length of time; and deterritorialising through the efforts of small groups of activists which move across enemy territory with one-off actions. Furthermore, these eco-protests underline the ways new 'geographies' are constructed while, at the same time, geography constructs social action, e.g. tree defences are of little use at quarries or underground tunnels are a less viable option at city street sites.

'Place' is usually understood as the location of direct experience, social action caught in an emotional whirlwind, in contrast to 'space' where social action is characterised by its rational construction, its self-reflexivity and mediated nature. The territorial action space of militant groups/action networks is the concrete location of both direct, face-to-face interaction and mediated interaction, of both the immediacy of emotions and the distance of reflexivity. However, its former features of direct interaction and collective 'effervescence' lend territorial space a significant tangibility and materiality for militant political struggle.

Paul Routledge (1997) further develops bell hooks' concept of "homeplace" as a social space — real, imaginary, and/or symbolic — which is constructed (however temporarily) so as to be at least partially insulated from control and surveillance in order that resistance can be organised and conceptualised. If we return our attention to the tenacious struggle on the part of activists in the 'Action Group Kynnefjället' we have another example of how places and resistances are mutually co-constitutive. Their small red cabin, isolated high on their mountain — their 'homeplace' of resistance — has infused their over 20 year long struggle with a 'structure of feeling' for the 'home' of their struggle, both the cabin and the mountain, which has become saturated with memories of resistance for the activists. For the activists involved, this snug and sheltered one room cabin has become the site of a mutually held definition of home. Their collective identity as eco-protesters has become over the years 'structured' by the cabin and the memories of protest and protesters sheltered by it.

While the concept of homeplace as a site for militant groups/action networks readily brings to mind a notion of a discrete territorial place, this place is cognitively mapped and is thus ambiguous in character. As Routledge (1997) points out, these homeplaces of resistance can be conceptualised as 'third spaces' in the terms of Homi Bhabha. That is:

> they are places where resistance is never a complete, unfractured practice, but rather places where practices of resistance are always entwined in some way with practices of domination such as marginalisation, segregation, or imposed exile. (p. 71)

In order to understand processes of militant political action it is necessary to understand how sites of resistance — homeplaces — are created, claimed, defended, and used. Routledge distinguishes between two spatial processes of homeplace construction and re-construction and the strategic mobility of resistance: movements of territorialisation and/or deterritorialisation. The former implies the temporary or permanent 'occupation' of place; the latter implies a movement across place. Routledge (1997) distinguishes between two spatial practices enacted within Nepal by the resistance movement during the 1990 revolution: those of the 'pack' and the 'swarm'. On the one hand, packs were small in numbers and subsequently did not directly confront dominating forces of power, rather they utilised tactics of surprise and unpredictability effecting a movement of deterritorialisation of space — moving across place, rather than occupying it. The raids conducted by small militant groups of animal rights protesters in Sweden, freeing minks from their farms or bombing a vivisection laboratory, are examples of packs. On the other hand, the swarm was large in numbers effecting a movement of territorialisation, directly confronting dominating powers by occupying (however temporarily) space by weight of their sheer numbers. (What I will later theorise as the militant contingent, see chapter three) And as Routledge argues, while the strategic mobility of resistance may constitute particular spaces as homeplaces, the material, symbolic and imaginary character of homeplaces will also influence the character of resistance. Places and resistances are mutually co-constitutive.

While both territorialisation and deterritorialisation are 'strategic' actions, they cannot be delimited on their own as sites of action from which opponents can be wholly excluded and challenged. 'Doors', points of possible intrusion in the 'homeplace' remain, however zealous their efforts to enclose the site for militant action. Hence, spatially, territorialisation and deterritorialisation are strategic sets of the tactics of militant groups undertaken always, however well hidden, within the opponent's field of vision. And lastly, these homeplaces are not bounded and stable, but are interconnected with broader (regional, national, international) processes and sites of resistance.

This brings us to a crucial point for understanding the action spaces of militancy on all three analytical levels; these action spaces are both unstable and penetrable. Their respective boundaries are not impregnable, opponents and critics can penetrate them through assault, nor are they impervious to the entry of possible supporters. These action spaces are not opaque, nor are they completely transparent. While the concrete walls of an occupied building may be the most manifest territorial action space, and a nation or 'turf' of a group, examples of less manifest territorial action spaces, all territorial action spaces, as are temporal and cognitive action spaces, while bounded, they are not impenetrable. They are more or less exclusive, but not solely exclusive. These action spaces, at all analytical levels, open towards the 'outside'. Through the 'door' of the occupied building, potential supporters may stream in, invited to engage in the social action taking 'place' there; or antagonists, the police or a rival social movement network of activists, may forge in, uninvited to this action space of 'place'; or the 'door' may even provide an avenue of quick retreat for the activists inside. (Cf. Ruddick, 1998)

Hence, actions spaces, whether understood cognitively, temporally, or territorially, are easily subjected to *hijacking*. An action space of militancy represents a field of opportunities, cognitive, temporal, and / or territorial, for the actions of other militant groups that are either antagonistic or compatible. They may be entered on invitation or by force, hence their bounds can just as easily be perceived by their points of entry, through the particularity of linkage *to* the 'outside', their linkages to social relations and practices beyond their 'boundaries'. In the following pages we will investigate the construction and reconstruction of the action spaces of militancy and their 'doors' by looking more closely at a specific case of militant political protest.

Militant Occupations: The Alingsås Brewery

Militant occupations, an often-used action form in Sweden, are explicit attempts to territorialise violence, even when the prescribed tactic of occupation is Gandhian non-violent civil disobedience. Violence — anticipated, threatened or actual — is an inherent feature of illegal occupations committed to the defence of a redefined space. Occupations are attempts to subordinate historical time to spatial enclosure; it is a militant tactic designed to intervene in history through the disruption of territory by processes of redefinition of the space of place. The interior of an occupied building, for example, is a space reserved for the ideological and material reproduction of a resistance community through violence — the construction of a 'homeplace' of resistance. The walls of the building and the barricades, the interface of the territorialised action space, are maintained as the prescribed place of violence. It is here, at the barricades and the walls, that the resistance community is entrenched and prepared to defend its action space against other rival militant groups and against the police.

Two activists explain the political challenge posed by occupations in the following words:

> [a]n occupation has always been, and will always be, an extreme form for direct action. It will always contribute to irritation and anxiety among the powerful and the establishment's people because an occupation hits them where it hurts most and is therefore most dangerous. The seat of power, rectification's and oppressions vital nerve and backbone — *private property rights* is challenged. (*Brand*, no. 1, 1996)

An occupation is an example of a territorial action space which is temporarily opened by tactics of territorialisation and where, as the two activists cited above pointed out, powers of domination are fundamentally challenged in that private property rights are defied. A building occupation is a territorial space strategically chosen and defended as one that offers some kind of latitude for independent social action. The occupation of an abandoned brewery in the small town of Alingsås, a few miles outside of Göteborg in Sweden, rapidly assumed the characteristic composite form of a temporary cognitive action space. Within the physical confines of the occupied building, a host of political groups and individuals come temporarily together. Bengt, a young activist in the Alingsås occupation, claims that "it is always the case with occupations, they attract all sorts of people". The occupation, which was initiated by SUF (Syndicalism Youth Federation) and Fältbiologerna ('Field Biologists', a youth environmental organisation) in protest against a municipal decision to tear the structure down to make way for a parking lot (the decision was taken despite a local referendum which voted for its restoration), opened a discrete territorial action space for groups and individuals to temporarily engage in a struggle which continually changed its goals and political formulation as new supporters entered its confines.

For many young people in Alingsås it was a concrete 'place' they could enter. Lars, who was 17 at the time of the occupation, explained that he was there in order to meet people. "There wasn't any other place we could meet." In the words of Jack, a young 17 year-old:

> I don't really know how I came to be engaged. It was really easy to come in there. I was confronted with a lot of new ideas, or new and new, they

were often ideas that I had before, but it felt as if I had come to people who felt just like me.

For many young people during the summer of 1996, the occupation offered them a concrete 'place' where they could find a sense of belonging, a collective sense of political purpose in response to what they perceived as oppression by the adult world's political institutions and norms. The abandoned brewery became a 'homeplace of resistance', invested with a 'structure of feeling' for the young activists who came to occupy its confines. Susanne, a 17 year-old, explained that their struggle over the brewery was a struggle "to secure a place to engage oneself and do things". Lisa, a 15 year-old activist, explained that they chose the tactic of occupation because:

> young people have no place in the parliamentary procedures. We have no voice; it is like we don't exist. ... The brewery was a place where young people governed collectively, with no leaders.

The original principles which guided the occupation — no leaders, no drugs, and no violence — although they were questioned and confronted they were widely accepted, but were not always inforced. While these three principles were their basic guidelines, it was important for them that given these basic principles or rules, everyone was welcome to enter into the action space. Thomas, a 21 year-old activist, emphasised that:

> it was something we emphasised all the time, that everyone was welcome and that everyone had as much right to make decisions, as long as they followed our basic principles. Of course one can't say that this is our brewery and these are the rules, instead these rules sort of grew out of our common meetings after our discussions. But what was important was that no one could come and feel like they were some sort of elite in this building, rather everyone was welcome to come and make their voices heard.

Most of the activists we interviewed emphasised the openness of their action space, however, as one activist pointed out, this ideal was both symbolically and in practice challenged by the construction of barricades on the part of the activists. He felt that barricades were not needed.

Those who sympathised with us were shut out and it made life inside the building more difficult. We constructed our own prison where at worst the lowest common denominator was more violence.

Within the 'encapsulation of space' by the brewery occupation this informant argued that discourses and practices of violence were enhanced. The situation created through the construction of barricades committed the resistance community to violence.

Within this territorial action space during the three months the occupation lasted these young activists were politically socialised, or rather, they socialised each other through countless meetings and group discussions. They progressively aligned their cognitive action space, their collective identity as militant squatters, with their territorial action space, the place of the brewery. Thomas claimed that if the young people were not politically engaged when they entered the occupation, they became so during the time they were there.

Linda, who was 15 at the time of the occupation, claims that not only the activists involved in the occupation, but the general population in the community of Alingsås and in particular the young people, became more and more critical of both politicians and police as the occupation progressed. According to this activist, democratic process, or rather the lack of, in their community was made visible in the struggle. She argued that in a small town like Alingsås political power lies in just a few hands and corruption is readily evident. All in all, she feels that as a result of the occupation "people in general became more critical and politically active".

Bengt has another view as to the collective political identity construction, the construction of their cognitive action space, which took place during the occupation. He claims that because of the youth of the activists, they became victims of an internal oppression in that they did not always dare say what they felt. There was an atmosphere surrounding the occupation, which placed a pressure upon the young people to take a militant stand.

Hannah explained that the lesson she learned from the occupation was a distrust in ideologies, what she called "ready-made packages", and the value of direct action in specific issues.

I think that it is much better to carry out direct actions in specific issues, like the brewery occupation, than to try and live in accordance with a utopia that is impossible to realise. All ideologies have enormous shortcomings. ... And as far as specific issues are concerned, sometimes you can even achieve some results. One can't make the whole world anarchist, at least I can't. There is too much work for too little result.

Hannah argues for the expediency of direct action, by 'doing' something in the here and now, one can intervene, at least in a small way, in history.

According to Bengt, an occupation attracts the most extreme political directions. The territorial action space opened by the occupation brought a wide range of groups and individuals on the far left to its action 'place'. In addition to young people from the Field Biologists, activists from the ultra-radical communist youth association from KPMLr, AFA (Anti-Fascist Action) activists, SUF (Syndicalism Youth Association) activists, and 'Chaotic Punks' assembled on the premises.

In addition to the activists that found themselves within the physical perimeters of the territorial action space, supporters clustered at the perimeters. It was primarily sympathisers to the occupation from the 'adult generation' that lent their support from the 'other side of the fence'. The action group, 'Friends of the Brewery', which had lobbied for a number of years for the preservation of the building, lent the young activists their support and even contributed financially. According to Susanne, they received unexpected support from the church that lent them chairs for the summer. After the attack on the brewery by neo-nazi youth, adults, primarily parents of the young occupants, began patrolling the perimeters. They had their own meetings and also arranged a meeting with the police where they vented their dissatisfaction with police methods to control the situation.

The perimeters of the territorial action space, the interface of violent action, even provided a temporary space for political dialogue among the citizens of this community. Jack tells about this space for dialogue:

it was actually kind of funny. When we stood guard on the roof we were visible for passers-by and we saw them. There is a sort of passage between the buildings. People always looked up and we heard what they said, even when they didn't think we heard. So we got a pretty good picture of who supported us and who didn't, what people thought about the occupation. But the prevailing attitude toward our occupation was positive, even if some yelled up, 'damn kids get out of there'. But our occupation at least got people talking here in Alingsås as things don't usually happen here.

However, the occupation was not only a territorial action space which attracted supporters within its confines, it also attracted antagonists to the occupation, and to the political groups within it. Aside from the coercive arm of the occupants' perceived adversaries — the politicians and the Businessmen's Association — the police who clamoured at the perimeters and eventually took control over the premises, the occupation attracted neo-nazi and racist youth groups to its action space. Neo-nazi groups posed a more or less constant threat for the occupants. Aside from minor provocations and harassment, their presence was more of a potential threat. However, on one occasion they organised their attack during which around 40 neo-nazi youths came, threw molotov cocktails at the windows and tried to enter the building. The occupants were highly critical of the police's actions, or rather non-action, on this occasion. Despite the fact that the police station was only a few hundred meters from the occupied building, it took the police more than two hours to arrive on the scene. And once there, they did nothing to remove their neo-nazi antagonists from the perimeters of the building. Nevertheless, this action on the part of the neo-nazi youth to hijack the territorial action space of the occupants resulted in a concrete goal of the occupation — a massmedial 'door' was opened to a broader public. For the first time the occupation attracted the attention of nation-wide mass media, both nation-wide newspapers and TV, through which the occupants could broadcast their struggle to a wider public.

Defining the Action — Mapping the Space

Within the confines of a physical action space, not only is a myriad of groups and individuals assembled, but even a myriad of political goals. What can begin as a simple political goal, in our case here, the preservation of a historical building, can, through the political process of ongoing negotiations and re-negotiations, emerge as a wide range of political goals. The initial goal is re-formulated: both expanded to include a more wide ranging critique and contracted or formulated more precisely as concrete alternative political measures. The contracted political reformulation became a demand to renovate the structure as a 'youth house', that is, premises for a wide range of youth activities. During the actual occupation this goal was realised — a cafe catering to the young people in the community was opened, a rave party was held, a number of punk bands held concerts, a folk music evening was organised and one evening they held a course in pre-modern Nordic dance. In addition, lectures were held on a range of topics: veganism, anti-nuclear power, non-violence, etc. According to Lars, "we did these things in order to show that a youth house could function and that there was a need for a place for the young people here".

The issues of the preservation of the actual structure, and the local community's measures for its young people, were soon reformulated as a broader question of democratic process in Alingsås. The initial struggle for the preservation of the brewery was fought out within the political system. On the basis of 2,500 collected signatures in the small community, they had managed to bring about a local referendum on the question, which those in favour of preservation won decidedly. However, the politicians claimed that the referendum had not engaged enough of the local population to be valid and over-turned this popular support for a restoration of the brewery and voted for its destruction in order to make way for the parking lot that the local Businessmen's Association demanded. The political context was set for both an occupation and its formulation in terms critical of the democratic process in the community. Lisa emphasised the occupation's goal of making visible the flaws in the democratic process of the community. They wanted to reveal for the public the principles that steered the town, which they perceived as serious departures from democratic rule. And most importantly they wished to make visible principles that should be inforced in a democratic society. In short, by 'living their utopia', they hoped to make visible a more democratic praxis. Almost all of the activists that we interviewed emphasised the importance of their principle of 'no leaders' and non-hierarchical structure. In order to counteract a hierarchy forming they practised direct democratic process with meetings where everyone present had a voice. Linda emphasised the importance of 'rounds' at the meetings so that everyone's voice could be heard. They attempted to follow the rule of consensus, which according to Thomas was successful, and which Bengt claimed was only a myth. Hannah, a 16 year-old activist, was more negative to these experiments in the direct democratic process. She claimed that too much of their meetings were taken up with meaningless talk and that consensus was in practice a sham in that oppositional voices were simply worn down by talk.

One of their guiding principles, that of 'no leaders', was practised in their self-proclaimed anti-hierarchical structure, however, Lars admitted that the activists who had been engaged longest wielded more influence than did 'new-comers' to the struggle. An informal cadre of leaders nevertheless emerged.

Underlying these more concrete innovations in democracy were the principles of inclusiveness — everyone was welcome to the territorial action space and could, in principle, engage on equal footing; and openness — all decisions made within the action space were open to discussions among all of the activists. In short, their occupation was an experiment in democratic process, and became a symbol of contrast to the democratic process they perceived in the wider society. They attempted to make visible a 'working' alternative to the 'Townhall pseudo-democracy' they perceived in Alingsås.

This construction of a 'lived utopia' in the here and now of the occupation held a particular significance for Lisa. This young activist emphasised time and again the importance of the alternative they collectively created during the occupation of the brewery:

> We wanted to create an activity, create a house for young people so that people could see that it works. That it isn't just something that one sits and talks about, that we could really make it work! That is what motivated our actions. ... We created a living house and it really did live! And there were a lot of people who saw that we could make things work. We had activities going on in the brewery for over a month before the occupation began ... a cafe, performances, public seminars and guided tours of the building and we cleaned and tidied up the place.

The Defence of Place

As in all militant political actions, where militancy is defined as a broach of the law resulting in other-directed, property-directed, and/or self-directed violence, the questions of violence contra non-violence, violence under what conditions, how 'much' violence, were heatedly debated. While the occupation had jointly decided upon the action principle of non-violence, the perimeters for this principle were an issue throughout the summer. For like all action 'principles' they must be negotiated and re-negotiated, defined and re-defined in each new action context.

When confrontation with the police authorities became a reality later during the summer, the issue of a non-violent action principle was again re-negotiated. Thomas relates his version of the events surrounding the preparations for tearing down the brewery:

> Sure we actively sought a confrontation with the police. We wanted to provoke a sort of focus for our struggle, keep the discussions alive. If for no other reason then in order to attract the media's attention. ... The provocation wasn't like ringing the police station with bomb threats, instead we threatened again and again that 'we won't budge, you'll have to throw us out'. Even if we weren't always sure ourselves if we wouldn't just leave if they started to throw teargas bombs at us. And then when they started to build the fence around the building, we started to fight. We dropped bottles from the windows, not so that they could injure anyone, but just to keep a tension in the air the whole time.

The action tactic described above was a clear attempt to focus the temporal action space by bringing the struggle to a 'head'. Thomas, as did the majority of activists we interviewed, interpreted the principle of Gandhian non-violence flexibly — violence under some conditions, against nazis in 'self-defence', and violence against property if the cause is good, and water or a carton of milk dumped on police officers as a temperate employment of violence to "provoke them a little" in order to bring a focus to their struggle.

Parallel with their 'defensive work', building barricades, arming themselves, negotiating and re-negotiating the tactics they would use against their adversaries, both their expected adversaries, the police, and their new adversaries who had intruded upon their action space, the neo-fascist youth groups, processes of 'definition work' or 'identity work' proceeded in the construction of their cognitive action space. In their 'defensive work', preparing themselves for confrontations with the police and neo-nazi youth, these young people were progressively 'militantised'. In other words, as the occupation progressed, their combativeness emerged as a collective identity. Even if they had negotiated collectively the principle of non-violence in their confrontations with the police, this principle was defined in ambivalent terms: "we just want to provoke them a little".

The Mass Media: A Point of Entry to the 'Outside World'

While Linda expressed reservations towards the media she pointed out that media is "a really good mouthpiece" for a political struggle. She claimed that the media played an important role in their recruitment of activists. For example, informations regarding a planned camp in non-violent protest received so to say free advertising through an interview with an activist on a regional radio station. According to Linda, in addition to information being spread through personal contact nets, the media played an important role in spreading information as to the occupation and its activities. Not only were potential supporters recruited by means of the media attention awarded the event, but the general public was informed as to goals of the occupation and made aware of what she claims were broaches of democratic process in the decision to tear the building down.

According to Thomas, they developed self-reflexive tactics for their dealings with media representatives. Media attention was rather weak during the early stages of their occupation, but Thomas felt that this was just as well. It gave them time to develop their own tactics for dealing with the media, and allowed them time to formulate the media messages they wished to spread. The most important media tactic was that journalists were always welcome in the building. Their tactic was to carry out their struggle publicly. In their meetings they discussed the points to be taken up at the press conferences they held. And they always met the media in a group, thereby actively avoiding media appointed leaders or spokesmen for the occupation. Nevertheless, according to Hannah, on several occasions the media appointed arbitrary leaders.

Other tactics were developed. They actively contacted the media and journalists that they felt were sympathetic to their struggle. According to Susanne, they made themselves available to the press in that they carried cellular phones. They photographed certain events and later on two occasions sold these photographs to the press. In particular they sought out the alternative left-wing press. According to Hannah, the most accurate accounts of their occupation were in these newspapers.

Their action tactics were incorporated in their media tactics. One of the reasons behind their temperate use of violence in their struggle was their concern for their media image; they did not want to appear to the public as unconstructive 'hooligans'.

When media interest waned, the activists took active measures to regain their interest. This was the goal of their occupation of the Townhall, a one-off action outside of their territorial action space, which they staged for a mass media audience. Through this media event, they were able to re-capture the media space, and make their demands and message heard. Lars tells about the event:

> when we occupied the Townhall we went in and took over all of the offices and raised our flag over the building. And then we called a lot of media from the building and motivated our actions by saying that no democratic decisions are taken anyhow in the Townhall. ... A picture from the occupation dominated the newsbills the following day. The police weren't involved, as they came to the conclusion that it was a public building until five o'clock. And we agreed not to use any violence or set up barricades, we couldn't afford to lose people that way anyhow. But it was a good way of getting the mass media there. ... We had held a number of press conferences at the brewery, but attendance had not been so good. But after this action we had more or less continuous attention from the press.

In summarising the occupation's relation to mass media it can be best described as one of friend *and* foe. (Cf. Peterson and Thörn, 2000) Thomas regarded the media as a potential, and necessary, partner in the struggle, and emphasised the need to develop reflexive tactics to both gain entry to media spaces and to influence the messages mediated within these spaces. The activists staged their occupation as a dramatic media performance. As the occupation progressed, they responded to the media with increasing savvy by developing tactics of media 'entry' (initiated contacts with journalists, supplied them with photographs from events) and to the best of their abilities they even attempted to manipulate the performative mechanisms of the media narratives, for example, by staging their one-off manifestation at the Townhall they brought their struggle 'to a head' and through the use of 'just enough violence' (dropping bottles and milk cartons from the roof of the beleaguered building), they also manipulated the 'pace of the action' with their temporal tactics of inducing a *tempo rubato,* a tempo of action 'stolen' from their adversaries, thereby providing the media narratives with a focus. Jack, Linda, Lars and Hannah had a more ambivalent perspective of the media's involvement in their occupation. While they were on the whole positive to the reports generated within the nation-wide media, they were highly critical of the local newspaper's coverage of their struggle. According to Jack, the newspaper published negative reports of the struggle, and 'shut off' further debate articles and letters to the editor which were critical towards the decision to tear down the brewery. "The local paper just ignored us and defamed our struggle". Jack touches upon an important factor in the ongoing struggle of social movements within media space. Established media industries also have economic interests. And a small local newspaper which is dependent upon the income they draw in from advertising will not be particularly willing to allow activists critical of small business interests free reign in their pages. If the media can act as a protagonist in a political struggle by providing a stage for the discursive duels fought by other protagonists, it can also be a protagonist by removing itself from the fray and denying the combatants a stage thereby instigating a so-called 'news blackout'.

A territorial action space of a militant group, in one of its most concrete senses, is perhaps the occupation of a building. Within its confines, the meaning of its social actions, its cognitive space, is temporally centred (for the duration of the occupation). Here militant protest is very concretely fencing off space as an attempt to define its own collective identity and the goals of their actions. However, this does not limit the scope of its actions which are most often directed outwards towards perceived adversaries and potential supporters beyond the walls of the occupied building. However, its collective identity construction crystallises within its confines, constructing there through spatial practices invested with meaning its vision of a better society, its lived utopia.

2 'Actions Speak Louder than Words': Durkheim and the *Magical Moment*

A new type of political violence among young people has begun to gain momentum throughout Europe. In earlier work I have argued that the explosive sociality of direct confrontation between rival social movement action groups and/or with the police riot squads is providing the cement for their collective identity construction. (Peterson 1995 and 1997) In this chapter I will discuss the contemporary phenomenon of the explosive sociality of militant political groups in contemporary complex societies in light of classical sociological theory. As early as 1903 Gustav Le Bon predicted that we were entering the "era of crowds", a phenomena of emotional intensity and potential revolutionary upheaval. (Le Bon, 1912) The phenomena in post-modern societies has been eloquently theorised in terms of "neo-tribalism" by Michel Maffesoli (1995) and Zygmunt Bauman (1993) as a societal process of expressive identity construction. Less eloquently, the phenomena has been discussed by Hans Magnus Enzenberger (1993) as the expression of mindless violence by roaming urban gangs (Cf. Peterson, 1994 for a critique) and bombastically theorised by Stepjan Mestrovic (1991) as post-modern forms of irrationalism, cynicism and disenchantment. (Cf. Peterson, 1996b for a critique) What insights can *fin de siécle* social theorists lend towards an understanding of collective identity formation among militant social movement groups and organisations today?

Emotions in Contemporary Social Movement Theory

The contemporary social movement theorist who has most systematically investigated the construction of collective identity in social movement action and paved the way for an analysis of emotions in collective identity construction is Italian sociologist Alberto Melucci. According to Melucci (1989):

> collective identity is an interactive and shared definition produced by several interacting individuals who are concerned with the orientations of their action as well as the field of opportunities and constraints in which their action takes place. (p. 34)

In short, it is the critical *we* of social action, the process whereby cognitive frameworks are formulated concerning the goals, means and environment of action; relationships are activated among the actors who communicate, negotiate and make decisions; and *emotional investments* are made which enable individuals to recognise themselves in each other.

In this chapter we will look more closely at these emotional bases for collective identity construction. In much of the social theorising of social movements since the latter 1960s, concerned with re-awarding collective action its so-called rational basis — a direct response to the social breakdown theorists of collective action which prevailed until they were challenged in the 1960s — the emotional bases for collective action have been more or less neglected. However, this neglect is in the process of being remedied in the theorising of contemporary collective action. (e.g. Alberoni, 1984; Robbins, 1988; Taylor and Rupp, 1993; Taylor and Whittier, 1992)

At the heart of British sociologist Kevin Hetherington's (1998) recent book is the very 'heart' of contemporary social movement politics — the emotional character of collective political processes of identification, what Hetherington calls "expressive identities". Hetherington argues that in the emotionally charged 'occasions' of events, both public and private within networks and groups, are to be found the loci of "a play between identity and identification" (p. 17) which links the cultural and political aspects of collective identities. Politics, according to Hetherington, is more than direct challenges lodged against the rationality of political-administrative systems. The so-called identity politics of social movements embrace both feeling and morality. Their everyday practices of solidarity construct them as political actors. They are 'emotional communities' as much as they are 'moral communities'; their overtly political moral protest is organised by the construction of emotional communities. In the succinct words of Hetherington:

[n]ew social movements and their wider lifestyle linkages offer not only a means of challenging powerful administrative systems morally, but also provide a form of affectual solidarity which allows — through the creation of distinct lifestyles, shared symbols and solidarity — a process of identity formation that seeks to develop a politics of difference and resistance through expressive means and forms of communication. It is not just the rationality of administrative systems, therefore, that is opposed by social movements, but also the supposedly inauthentic, disenchanted instrumentality of interpersonal relations embedded in a routinised, often unjust, everyday life. (p. 37)

It is the role of feeling in social movement politics that is the focus of Hetherington's project.[1] In other words, it is the situated and specific practices of expressive identities — the organisation of emotions — which is at the centre of his analysis.

Ron Eyerman and Andrew Jamison (1998) discuss in their latest book *Music and Social Movements* the reciprocal and mutually reinforcing relations between social movements and popular culture. That in addition to ideology and social theory, or as will be argued here, not only in addition, but more than ideology and social theory, i.e. 'talk', popular music also:

provides a sense of belongingness, a sharing in a collective vision, by making use of more emotive language and rhythms — and innovative performance practices that linked the musical and the political. (p. 138)

Music in a sense is a structure of feeling, which, according to these theorists, can communicate a feeling of common purpose. The cultural praxis of social movements, for example, their music-making as innovative forms of understanding, as truth-bearing cognitive structures, what Eyerman and Jamison call exemplary action, not only provides the bonding substance which holds social movements together with a sense of common purpose or identity, but also impact upon and are capable of transforming wider, established cultures. Exemplary action as a form of communicative action "aims at communicating a vision of what the world could be like to others. (p. 172)" In doing so, exemplary action embodies the meaning of a social movement.

1 Hetherington rejects the use of what he calls denotative terms like 'social movements' and "their Hegelian totalising heritage", preferring to deconstruct them and examine "the fragments that make up the mulitiplicity that remains". (p. 9)

Central to their arguments in this text is the notion of tradition that they re-evaluate and re-introduce into a sociological analysis. Eyerman and Jamison argue that:

> [t]radition, the past in the present, is vital to our understanding and interpretation of who we are and what we are meant to do. As such, it is a powerful source of inspiration for social movements and emergent cultural formations. These include most obviously traditions of protest and rebellion, but also, more subtly, forms of living and underlying sensibilities, which still exist in the residues and margins of society. Such structures of feeling can be embodied and preserved in and through music, which is partly why music is such a powerful force in social movements and in social life generally. (p. 161)

The communication of traditions through cultural praxis, what we have called collective learning processes (Peterson and Thörn, 1994), works on two levels according to these authors. Firstly, on a deep-rooted, anthropological level at which reality is interpreted and experienced, traditions and rituals (which as symbolically pregnant performances embody the ideas and orientations contained in traditions) provide bridges between movements and generations. Secondly, on an aesthetic level, cultural expression and innovation transforms traditions into living sources of collective identity.

Why have Eyerman and Jamison chosen to highlight tradition in their analysis, thereby contributing to an ongoing revaluation of the notion for the social sciences, which have for so long relegated tradition in the modernisation paradigm to the dustbin of acceptable concepts? The title of one of their chapters, 'Taking traditions seriously', could just as well have been titled 'Taking emotions seriously'. For repeatedly in their text they emphasise the 'emotive force' of cultural praxis, a force which reaches deeper and beyond rational discourse or talk, activating and re-activating profoundly lived and living experiences, which so successfully communicates a collective identity, a sense of common purpose in collective political action. (Cf. Peterson, 1997a: chapter three)

> The difference between culture and science ... is that the exemplary action of music and art is lived as well as thought: it is cognitive, but also draws on more emotive aspects of human consciousness. As cultural expression, exemplary action is self-revealing and thus a symbolic representation of the individual and the collective which are the movement. (p. 22)

And if the notion of tradition has been so rudely neglected in the social sciences, have not emotions been equally neglected by a social science so thoroughly submerged in the discourse of rationality?

Sociologist Eugene Halton in his book *Bereft of Reason* (1995) has headlong tackled this latter question. In this book he submits a 'biosemiotic social theory', inspired by the philosophical pragmatism of Charles Pierce, the vast works of social critique of Lewis Mumford, and the anthropological 'listening' of social dramas by Victor Turner, which is:

> capable of encompassing both the varieties and contingencies of human signification and the organic needs, limits, and transformative possibilities of the living human being in his and her social, political, and economic worlds, forms a profound critique of contemporary theory and contemporary life, and of the spirit of mechanised, depersonalised subjectivism which informs both. (p. 277)

In short, Halton is reinjecting the body, emotions, and lived/living experiences in contemporary social theory that with its 'rationalist' blindfold has divorced emotions and lived bodied experience from its horizon of concerns. At the centre of his arguments is a doctrine of human emotions that posits that:

> human emotions are the chief vehicles for the practice of everyday life — or, in semiotic lingo — emotions are a principle mode of semeiosis or communicative practices in the conduct of life, operating at a level significantly different from that of rational discourse, a level more basic than rational or linguistic discourse or critical thought, and one which provides the tonal ground of rational discourse. (p. 259)

Halton passionately advocates a 'real *Homo sentimentalis*' which encompasses both the human ability to feel one's way in the world and with others empathetically, as well as the human ability to idealise emotions, to make them the servants of ideas. In this latter sense, perhaps Eyerman and Jamison's exemplary 'intellectual artists' are so successful in embodying the vision of a movement through the exemplary cultural actions of their songs, in that they have the human ability to idealise emotions, making them the servants of collectively held ideas. The collective meaning construction of social movements, in Halton's terms, is not a fundamental rational process, and the finding and resolving of problems through reasonable, communicative means is not restricted to rationally linguistic validity claims but is an in-built facet and potential of human experience — rationality is neither the chief nor the sole arbiter of human conduct. In this vein, Halton, too, turns his attention to tradition — tradition, as it was conceptualised in the early 20th century work of 'philosophical anthropologist' Max Scheler, as non-instinctive deep-seated social forms of learning. According to Halton:

> we have begun to reengage tradition as a potentially vital source for contemporary life, ranging from the widespread revival of religious life, to the reengagement of the arts with the past, to the scientific interest in traditional agriculture, diet, and knowledge of plants. (p. 53)

Traditions, for Halton, remain, while sublimated and even repressed by the reflective consciousness of modernity, as a potential reservoir of cultural energies, for good or bad. It is the emotive force of the lived, bodied experiences transmitted through tradition which can be re-actualised by social movements in their learning processes connecting the past with the present which is the source of cultural energies or cultural transformation. For Hetherington (1998) it is the tradition of Romanticism, more specifically, the romantic critique of modern societies, which is the basis of contemporary social movements' expressive identity politics. The traditions of Romanticism, reactualised by social movements, offer an aesthetic outlook on the world rather than one defined solely by science and rationality. Romanticism focuses on issues of individual lived/living experience and the emotionality of 'occasions' and through "political activity, the romantic seeks to express him or herself as a moral agent". (p. 77)

Eyerman and Jamison's (1998) work also helps to fill the gap within contemporary social movement theory which says much about rational talkers talking but very little about actors acting: felt, perceptive, imaginative, bodily experiences do not fit into the prevailing theories of social movement's communicative actions. The profoundly held beliefs advocated by social movements which grip our lives cannot be solely founded on rationality, for the rational alone is too meagre and rootless to act as inspiration for enduring belief's, such beliefs "have to be rooted in life itself". (Halton, 1995: 166) Eyerman's and Jamison's work on music and social movements addresses that gap by showing the ways in which the exemplary actions of music-making in social movements roots beliefs to emotive life sources. Hetherington's theorising on the expressive nature of collective identity construction, its emotionally lived/living basis, bridges the political and cultural aspects of social movement politics. These theorists shed light upon the processes whereby emotions are the bearers of traditions in collective action.

In my own work I have sought to examine how ritual confrontations have generated emotional states which are a fundamental basis for the collective identity construction among militant political groups/action networks. It is in this context that I have discussed what I termed *neo-sectarianism* — phenomena not new or unique to contemporary societies approaching the *fin du millennium*, but one that even preoccupied the social critics and analysts of modernity at the *fin de siécle*. Neo-sectarianism, the highly exclusive collective identity construction of militant high-risk political groups/action networks is just one tendency or direction inherent in contemporary political protest (together with the construction of highly inclusive and tentative 'rainbow coalitions'). In Peterson (1997a and 1995) I analysed the collective identity construction of militant groups, what I designate there as neo-sects, on the basis of three fundamental mechanisms for group 'fusion': ideology, cultural praxis, and confrontation. I placed emphasis upon the interactive processes of conflict, i.e. ritual confrontation, which fosters a mentality of embattlement creating a vision of the world as divided between 'we' and 'them'. I argue that this mentality of embattlement is particularly enhanced by their lived experiences of physical confrontations with their adversaries, be these confrontations with the police, military, or other youth groups. Radicalisation and group fusion follow the everyday emotionally and bodily lived experiences of conflict and turmoil on the part of militants in their action spaces.

But why designate the contemporary political phenomena of militant, high-risk, exclusive political groups as neo-sects? Why exchange Maffesoli's notion of the neo-tribe with the more classical term sect that is laden with religious connotations? I argue that neo-sect is a more appropriate metaphorical concept than neo-tribe to describe the restless products of explosive 'political' sociality. The 'tribe' is a unit that is based on vital, existential ties of physical proximity; one is 'born' into a tribe. (See Peterson, 1997a) A sect is based on voluntary participation and is not necessarily dependent upon physical proximity. Sects in classical sociological theory, for example in the work of Max Weber, were small, relatively loosely organised, religious groups of committed believers whose members actively joined them in order to further their beliefs. They usually were set up in protest against a church and tended to withdraw from the surrounding society into communities of their own. Michel Maffesoli (1996), while he prefers the metaphorical concept of neo-tribe paradoxically emphasises the 'religious model' for understanding contemporary 'groupism'. Etymologically, the word religion (religare) alludes in its broadest sense to *reliance,* and is a useful way of understanding the nature of the bonding and its moral potential within contemporary micro-groups. He points out that the present, proximity, the feeling of being part of the group, responsibility — so many of the characteristics of what he calls neo-tribes are at work in the sect-group. The neo-sect is a contemporary moral community in the Durkheimian sense, where moral does not allude to 'morally correct', but to an intensely felt sense of 'we'.

The Neo-Sect and its Theoretical Inspiration

The notion of the neo-sect builds upon the theoretical conceptualisation of Hermann Schmalenbach, a student of Simmels. Herman Schmalenbach (1885 - 1950) published in 1922 a critique of Ferdinand Tönnies dual concepts of *Gesellschaft* and *Gemeinschaft,* adding a third category, the *Bund,* which is of central importance for our continued discussion. (On Schmalenbach see further Peterson, 1997 and 1998; and Hetherington, 1994 and 1998) Edward Shils (1957) claims that Schmalenbach's essay was the first stage in the turning away from the uncritical contrast between *Gemeinschaft* and *Gesellschaft,* or primary group and the atomised large-scale society. In regards to the concept of sect, Schmalenbach (1977 [1922]) criticises Max Weber for not drawing out the consequences of Ernest Troeltsch's (1931) important distinction between church and sect, where church is a community (*Gemeinschaft*) which can develop into society (*Gesellschaft*) and a sect which is a *pure communion (Bund).* According to Schmalenbach, instead of exploiting this distinction and transforming the basic dichotomical categories of sociology lanced by Tönnies into a necessary trichotomy, he held fast to his point of departure in the dichotomy. This despite the fact that Weber distinguished, within community, between traditional and affective or emotional bonds. The latter form of community (communion)[2] – that which is borne along by waves of emotion, "reaching estatic heights of collective enthusiasm, rising from the depths of love or hate" (p. 332) — is relegated, in Max Weber's formulation, to a subform of community. Schmalenbach counters and argues that communion is an alternative social form altogether, differing both from community and society.

Firstly, for Schmalenbach, community, society and communion are general and modal categories, rather than constituting species of concrete structures, such as the 'bourgeoisie', the 'clan' or the 'family'. They are *forms of being* that may or may not be assumed by concrete structures. Secondly, these three modal forms are reciprocally interrelated; they sustain a mutual dependence. For example, the very relations of society and communion required for their existence elements of community such as language, shared values, or other shared commonalties that are given by nature. By the same logic, communion and community cannot persist in the absence of societal forces. And lastly, community and society arise out of the conditions of communion. In short, the one social form does not replace the other. Change is not perceived in the unilinear sense of Tönnies, but in a more cyclical view, which oscillates between institutionalisation and rejuvenation.[3] Society does not develop in a simple or straightforward line from community. For example, he argues that a specific ethos underlies society, and that ethos, especially when it first appears, may be consolidated by communion. Schmalenbach (1977) goes on to typologise historically specific eras as having different interrelationships between these three modal forms, with one of the forms assuming a position of predominance. The Western world that Schmalenbach

2 'Bund', the translaters selected Cooley's term, communion, for this form of human association in a somewhat arbitrary and forced effort to establish some continuity between American and German thinking on these matters.

3 Erik Cohen (1983) has applied Schmalenbach's model in an analysis of the structural transformations of the kibbutz. He investigates phylogenetically the historical process of transformation from the Bund to the 'Commune' (Gemeinschaft) to the largest and most mature kibbutzim, the 'Association' (Gesellschaft). However, this is a radical departure and missapplication from Schmalenbach's model which does not advocate a phylogenetical path of development, on the contrary, Schmalenbach's model is fundamentally non-linear and non-evolutionary.

lived in he regarded as being dominated by the society form, just as was the case, according to Schmalenbach, in ancient Greece.

Now that we have reviewed the epistemological nature of Schmalenbach's three social forms, let us go on to investigate their distinctive definitions.   In regards to society, his least developed category, its essential character, in contrast with community, lies in the priority of individual over social existence.   Society refers to those relations that are entered into by previously unrelated individuals and these constitutive relations involve reciprocity:

> every action as a rule takes place on behalf of some counter action and in the expectation of it. *Contract* is representative of society. (p. 339, my emphasis) The relations are visible and hence rational, just as the totality of societal relations is only indeed a relational matter. The spirit of society is inspired by the ethos of a cool reserve. (ibid.)

In contrast to society, the members of community are originally interdependent, the natural or communal bonds are enduring, i.e. one cannot leave one's family in any real sense.   Spatial and temporal contiguity, according to Schmalenbach, is an essential basis of that order of coalescence that we call community.   The distinguishing characteristics of community are the natural qualities of its basis and the fact that only communities have such natural bases that are simply taken for granted.   Schmalenbach clarifies this taken-for-grantedness in the following manner:

> community implies the recognition of something taken for granted and the assertion of the self-evident. ... One is usually not fully aware of them [communities]. They are given. They simply exist. As a rule we are not likely to take much notice of our membership in them, even when it is a question of our membership in far-flung communities — such as commonalties of language, of ethnicity, or of the fact of a common humanity. The communal circles of which we are part reach into imponderable distances and cover connections of all kinds. One can not be aware of all of them. Yet, as persons, they always affect us. Our own unconscious is directly or indirectly constituted in and through them. Only through contrasts and disturbances does a community become an object of attention for its members. (p. 334)

Communion, or in Schmalenbach's own terminology, the 'Bund', in contrast to community, is an entirely different matter. A Bund is elective, not ascriptive as is the case of community; the bonds that hold its members together have neither 'natural bases' nor can they be taken-for-granted. According to Shils (1957), Schmalenbach delved into Tönnies concept of *Gemeinschaft* and discerned a diversity of phenomena.

> He saw that it was possible for a state of intense and comprehensive solidarity to exist without those who shared it possessing either a common territory of origin and residence, a common place of work or ties of blood and sexual connection. When these primordial elements were isolated from the original concept of *Gemeinschaft*, the residue was the *Bund*, for which such terms as confraternity, brotherhood, league, band, gang are all poor translations but each of which brings to the fore the element of intense mutual attachment, independent of primordial ties. (Shils, 1957:133-134)

Shils, on his part, delved into Schmalenbach's concept of Bund and discerned two separate, while related, phenomena — the "ideological Bund" and the "personal Bund". While both forms of Bund are integrated through common attachments to values or beliefs, in the "ideological Bund" the value emphasis is on the tasks of the Bund in the world beyond its community; it has a political message it wishes to convey to society. In the "personal Bund" the value emphasis is turned principally to the community itself — to the ideals of human relationships the members are expected to live up to.

The bonds of the Bund must be continually asserted and reasserted, *enacted*, for the form of sociality of the Bund is a direct result of social acts and cannot persist outside of these social acts. Subsequently, in contrast to the enduring bonds of community, the bonds of communion, the 'Bund', are tentative and its structure is inherently unstable. Schmalenbach argues that Bunds always tend to become transformed into either societal or communal structures as they either break up or are routinised. He exemplifies these processes with the transformation of sects (Bund) into churches (society), and the Bund of heterosexual love into the community of marriage and the family.

Schmalenbach emphasises that the 'Bund' is a sociation of *fusion*, rather than of *coalescence* as is the case with community, or *contract* as is the case of society, which further underlines the brittle and tentative character of the 'Bund'. In the zestful words of Schmalenbach (1961):

> [t]he character of human communion requires fairly intense mutual

involvement, and the emotional ecstasy on which communion depends is a fleeting thing. The emotions come and go like tides of the sea. Their power may be great. They can shake us to the very root, destroy us, or even drive us to distraction or madness, but they do not endure. (p. 340)

Central to Schmalenbach's perception of the 'Bund' as a form of sociation is the state of emotional intensity that is its basis. Its members 'fuse', go up in the common cause of their association — strongly and passionately held universal values or beliefs. It is in this sense of fusion, what Gurvitch (1941) was later to call 'states of collective ecstasy', as a crucial moment in the construction of the bund, or what I designate as the sect, that the connections to the sociology of Émile Durkheim are readily observed, particularly in connection with Durkheim's (1965: 139ff) notion of *collective effervescence.*

The explicit use of the notion of sect in political analysis has a precedent in an early work of American sociologist Howard Becker. Howard Becker (1946) was the first, in my knowledge, to use the concept of sect in analysing the secular phenomena of social movement revolt in his study of the German youth movement, the so-called 'Roamers' or 'Wandervogel', from the 1890s until the outbreak of World War II. According to Becker:

> like-mindedness resulting from dissent, from rejection of adult standards, gave rise in Germany to little conventicles which later fused into sects. If a boy or girl had developed a personality making association on the basis of like-mindedness congenial, it was then possible for him or her to join forces with other rebels against a despised adult way of life. (pp. 40-41)

Becker argues that in a very real sense the Roamers met the requirements, which the student of the religious structures of Western Christendom sets up for his sect definition. Becker maintains that:

> [i]t is a relatively small plurality pattern that has abandoned the attempt to win the whole world over to its ... [way of life]; the phrase 'Come yea out from among them and be yea separate' is followed literally. It is readily seen that the sect is a ... body which one must *join* in order to become a member; [it is *elective*] At the bottom, the sect is [*exclusive* in character], appeals to strictly personal trends, and frequently requires some definite type of ... *experience as a prerequisite of acceptance.* It therefore attaches primary importance to the religious experience [broadly interpreted] of its members prior to their fellowship. ... It frequently *rejects an official clergy,* preferring

to trust for guidance to lay inspiration rather than to trained expertness. In many instances sects are persecuted, but this persecution only reinforces the *separatist and semi-ascetic attitude* toward the world inherent in the sect as a social structure. At times it ... seeks to sever as much as possible the bonds which tie it to the common life of the larger ... [society] within which it develops. In general, the *sect prefers isolation to compromise.* (p. 83, my emphasis) [e.g. Ernst Troeltsch's (1931) definition of sect, p. 166]

Pushing his 'religious line of analysis' further, Becker extends the conceptual framework to include *the denomination* and *the ecclesia.* The early Roamer sects, despite their similarity, clung to their own nests and their own supposedly peculiar sense of fusion. First in 1913, on the hill of Hohe Meissner, over 3,000 representatives gathered, and "whipped to revival fervour by the moving speeches of their leaders" (Becker, 1946: 100), nearly all the sects merged into an overarching union called Free German Youth. No longer basically without goals in their social actions, they became welded together in a search for a new value-system and a belief in the vague notion of 'the folk community', and after the shattering impact of World War I the folk community came more and more to represent the one thing which was so desperately needed. At this point the Roamers assumed the traits of, in Becker's conceptual framework, a denomination. In Becker's terms, denominations are simply sects in an advanced stage of development and adjustment to each other and the secular world. Lost is the early fervour of the self-conscious sect. According to Becker (1946) "age inevitably brings the denominational compromise". (p. 149)

The ground was laid for the emergence of Nazism within the German youth movement. Becker goes on to argue that the Nazi Party was originally a cult which rapidly became a sect. However, Nazism was a sect with a special difference:

for instead of isolating itself from the elements in German life antagonistic to it, there was from the beginning the iron resolve to convert all doubters to the One True Faith. Sect was envisaged as potential *ecclesia* from the start [professedly universal in its aims]. (p. 168)

What developed was an all-encompassing State Church or ecclesia devoted to the perpetuation of the value-system of Nazism. Leadership within the youth movement shifted from an authority based on personal charisma (the sect) to the charisma of office. The authority of youth leaders was the charisma of office supported by a highly institutionalised ecclesia — they were awarded a share of Hitler's charisma.

Becker's analysis gives further credence to the notion of sect, understood in Shils (1957) terms as "ideological bund", as a designation for highly exclusive, militant social movement groups/action networks. However, the role emotions play in the construction of these groups remains unclear. So if the role of emotions in the political processes of social movements has not been entirely neglected by sociologists — both earlier and contemporary — it has nevertheless all too often been relegated to a 'supporting role' in the drama of politics. In this chapter I will further engage with the role of emotions in militant actions, that actions 'speak louder than words' because of the emotive force they leash and unleash. In focus in the remaining pages is the work of Émile Durkheim for an understanding of the contemporary forms of political 'groupism', *sic* neo-sectarianism, emerging. But before we investigate the saliency of the work of Durkheim for the phenomena of neo-sectarianism, we will look more closely at the phenomena in question — political militancy in contemporary Sweden. Firstly, a general overview will be presented as to the extent of militant political groups' confrontations with authorities and/or other militant groups in high-risk illegal actions, together with examplifications of the types of illegal high-risk actions being carried out by militant left-wing action groups in Sweden. What is the phenomenon we are theorising in terms of the emotive force of confrontations? Secondly, we will compare this wave of social movement militancy of groups on the political 'left' with one of its historical social movement antecedents — the Swedish Anti-Vietnam War Movement, *FNL*. What distinguishes militant collective action today in Sweden from its historical antecedents?

Militant Groups Confronting the Authorities

The Swedish Intelligence Agency (SÄPO) has made a survey of politically motivated crimes in Sweden, which since 1994 has provided more reliable statistics over crimes connected with political movements. (*Brottslighet kopplad till rikets inre säkerhet under 1994/1995; Brottslighet kopplad till rikets inre säkerhet under 1995/1996* and *Brottslighet kopplad till rikets inre säkerhet under 1997*) According to their surveys, the vast majority of crimes of this character have been carried out by groups and individuals directly or indirectly connected to racist organisations and movements on the far-right, around 1,500 crimes committed during 1995 and during 1997 1438 of a total of 2736 reported politically motivated crimes. Thereafter followed politically motivated crimes which were more or less connected to what they designate as 'the autonoma network' (an anarchist network on the far-left of the Swedish political spectrum), around 100 crimes committed during 1995. However, since 1995 the number of reported criminal acts committed by militant activists with far-left sympathies has risen dramatically. The statistics for 1997 were broken down further and reported 340 crimes committed by animal rights activists, 84 attacks against Shell Service stations, 48 crimes committed by feminist activists, 27 crimes committed by road-protesters, and 113 miscellaneous left-orientated criminal actions. Furthermore, the number of criminal attacks which the 'autonoma' and right-wing extremists direct towards each other appear to be balanced between them.

According to these reports, the suspects were primarily in the age group 15 to 19 years old, followed by the age group 20 to 24 years old among both racist and right-wing extremist crimes and crimes carried out in connection with left-wing extremism. However, while right-wing extremist criminality was almost exclusively a male activity, the number of female suspects in left-wing criminal acts was almost equal that of male suspects. Another difference in the suspect profile of these two groups in their material was that the majority of left-wing suspects had no previous record, and if they did, their previous criminal charges also had a political background. In contrast, more than half of the suspects in right-wing related criminal acts had a criminal record, often including several charges, which were without any political motivation, primarily car theft, use of a vehicle without lawful authority, and/or assault charges.

According to SÄPO, the difference between the types of crimes committed by these 'political extremists' was largely the degree of their organisation. Crimes carried out by activists from the far-left were directly linked to political decisions and campaigns instigated by political groups and action networks. Their actions tended to be well planned and most often were part of a systematic campaign against what they defined as a political relevant phenomenon in society, e.g. racism, Swedish arms production and export, the spread of pornography and sexism in general, the 'inhuman' treatment of animals, the construction of an extended highway system in Stockholm — the so-called 'Dennis Package', and multinational companies' exploitation of third world countries, more specifically, Shell Oil's support of the military dictatorship in Angola. The far-right movement in Sweden rests upon a more unstable ground, dependent upon the large number of sympathisers on the periphery of their highly organised nucleus, mainly young skinheads. Subsequently, the far-right crimes had a more 'spontaneous' and unorganised character; nevertheless, these crimes were often extremely serious, including, for example, during 1995: three murders, 46 cases of assault and battery, and at least 100 other serious crimes of other-directed violence. Around a quarter of the crimes reported with racist or right wing extremist character were indirect threats towards immigrants in their homes, which were conveyed either per telephone or per post. 75% of the crimes committed by right-wing extremists were committed against individuals with immigrant backgrounds and refugee centres. All in all, the vast majority of right-wing motivated crimes were committed against persons, in contrast with the majority of left-wing motivated crimes, which were committed against property. These types of crimes included in 1995 property damages towards Shell stations including arson attacks; property damages against pornoshops; the widespread attacks by animal rights activists against meat-packers and furriers, hot dog stands, laboratories, mink farms, and 'egg factories', which included bombings, arson attacks, and the 'liberation' of laboratory animals, chickens and minks; illegal demonstrations against the 'Dennis Package' and property damages against road construction machinery in Stockholm; and, illegal entry of SAAB:s grounds in Linköping (the manufacturer of the military attack plane JAS 39 Gripen) and sabotage (the 1994 sabotage of the nosecone of a SAAB Viggen jet at the military airfield in Såtenäs). Antifascist action groups diverged from this pattern of left-wing criminality against property to include acts of violence directed towards persons, primarily against police and right-wing activists, during large demonstrations. Furthermore, a trend has been observed within the animal rights movement that an increasing number of unlawful threats against individuals and companies have been reported since 1996. Increasingly, violence — self-directed, other-directed, and/or property-directed — has entered the alternative left-wing political culture in Sweden.

These surveys by the Swedish Intelligence Agency over criminal politically motivated acts provide us with an overview of contemporary political militancy in Sweden; however, its records of left-wing political violence would appear to be somewhat abbreviated. Left-wing activists report in their own media outlets (left-wing newspapers and Internet home-pages) far more illegal political actions than what appears in SÄPO's survey, as well as reporting a far greater diversification of action strategies, the variegated political issues addressed by these actions, and the broad variation of sites for politically motivated actions. In the following pages I will attempt to capture this diversification of political militancy on the part of the left wing as reported by the activists themselves.

Leftist Action Groups 'Taking Action'

On 20 December 1995 approximately 20 activists, from several action groups, occupied a subway station in Stockholm to protest the construction of the 'northern link' in the highway construction circling Stockholm, the so-called 'Dennis Package'. They began their occupation an hour before the scheduled closing of the station (the station was closed for several months in the early evening due to tunnel blasting) by engaging subway passengers in a 'party'. They sold Christmas soft drinks, buns and ginger cookies, played music and handed out flyers. At the designated time for evacuation, four of the activists chained themselves at the station and a police riot squad dragged over 20 activists out for police questioning. According to Mikael:

> we are trying to hold the University's subway station open and therefore we are inviting passengers to a party on the platform. In this way we are protesting against the Dennis package's indefensible staking of mass motorism. We hope that the action can lead to a series of actions at the station which can subsequently hinder the nightly blasting. (*Brand*, no. 1, 1996)

On 17 February 1996 three activists carried out a sabotage action against the highway construction project in Stockholm. Three construction machines and the electric system were sabotaged; protest messages were spray-painted on the wall of a tunnel. (*Brand*, no. 5, 1996) In February 1996, the action group, 'Social Ecological Action', occupied the Communications Offices for the 'Dennis Agreement' for one day. They welcomed all interested passers-by to visit the premises. According to the group, their goal is to improve the quality of information released by the offices. They argue that the office's budget of ten million crones each year are spent to spread propaganda supporting the highway project and to subsequently silence the critique the project has evoked. (*Brand,* no. 2, 1996)

In early May, 1996 a building contractor's premises was occupied by several actions groups calling themselves 'Friendship Groups Against Dennis' in protest against the highway project. While the occupation was civil disobedient and they were eventually evacuated by the police and charged with unlawful entry, they employed the Gandhian principle of non-violence. The objective of their symbolic action was to make visible the struggle, arguing that, "there hasn't been either an open debate or referendum in the issue, despite that the Dennis Package is the largest venture in the history of Stockholm's communication network." (*Brand,* no. 3, 1996) Later in the month, the same action groups carried out another attack on the premises, this time with the goal of "more active resistance". The office's maps were burned and Coca-Cola was poured in the computers. (*Brand,* no. 3, 1996) The friendship groups carried out a series of actions during late spring 1996. In addition to the above-mentioned occupations, they held a symbolic picnic on a motorway wearing gasmasks. They opened a symbolical environmental customs station outside the regional government offices. They held a week-long tent camp outside the same offices. They constructed a sandbox equipped with toy cars outside of the highway administration offices. Some 'tree-huggers' managed to delay construction while the police waited for the fire department to remove the activists. Approx. 150 activists blockaded construction machines, delaying work for about five hours.

Olle Meurling, writes about the organisational process in the struggle against the Dennis Package. According to Meurling, for several years action groups had been carrying out protest actions against the highway project in Stockholm, but the activities had followed the usual cycles: while the concrete actions had gathered a number of activists, few stayed on to organise and co-ordinate the continuous work. Slowly activists became aware of the need for organisation and a meeting was held in April 1996 with this express purpose during which nine 'friendship groups against Dennis' were formed. According to Meurling, organising themselves in friendship groups has allowed more activists a voice in the planning of actions. Within the groups, activists have been able to prepare themselves for action through discussions around fear, what happens in the event of arrest, how to deal with the media, as well as train themselves in various action situations. Meurling claims that these action preparations have given the activists a greater sense of security. The friendship groups are relatively autonomous and they decide themselves what action strategies that they will employ. However, "when we carry out actions together we have agreed upon a strategy of open civil disobedience". (*Brand*, no. 3, 1996) Meurling writes that a division of responsibility or function has spontaneously developed among the friendship groups. Some of the groups have chosen to play the part of support groups for the groups that actually carry out the action. For example, during the two occupations of the building contractor's premises, the support groups remained outside, passed out flyers explaining the action and took contact with the press, and through song and music gave their support to their comrades within the building. After the action, they gathered outside the police station waiting for the release of the arrested activists. In regards to the question of secrecy, Meurling claims that all of the arrested activists have remained silent during police questioning as to how the actions have been organised and prepared. However, the actual actions have been carried out as open civil disobedience, which has resulted in good media publicity around the actions. While most of the actions of the friendship groups have had a symbolical protest character, some have been more directed towards direct resistance, for example, the above-mentioned occupation. Meurling points out that not all of the activists involved in the friendship groups are anarchists, some are "simply environmental activists, unorganised activists or from other left organisations". He writes that the purpose of the friendship groups is to function as an action arm of the established Dennis opposition's network, 'Ur Tid Är Leden'.

The question of sabotage actions is a bone of contention for the Friendship Group network. According to Meurling, the groups have full autonomy and can use whatever action forms they wish, however, in the case of sabotage actions "they cannot use our common name". He writes that the goal of all of their actions is to encourage others to engage themselves in extra-parliamentary action in the struggle to stop the highway project. He says that in order to increase our numbers and bring about a halt in the project:

we must see through and confront the urban vision which underlies the 'Dennis Package'. We must build broad alliances with various social movements and in line with the healthcare employees union, we must link the 'Dennis Package' to other pressing urban questions. In the end it is a question as to what sort of city we wish to live in. The 'Dennis Package' can not be reduced to an environmental threat. Its underlying purpose is to create a 'new' Stockholm for the interests of power. (Ibid.)

The umbrella organisation, 'Actions to Stop the Bridge', gathered approx. 600 demonstrators against the bridge project in a protest demonstration on 9 March 1996 outside Malmö. The otherwise peaceful demonstration divided when several hundred activists spontaneously marched to the bridge foundations on the Swedish side. They were met by a massive police riot squad and were dispersed. However, according to some of the more militant activists, the unsuccessful attempt to break into the restricted area was an important 'learning experience' for many, making explicit, they argued, that the police were their primary enemy and the necessity of holding a united front, both physically and cognitively, as well as underlined the necessity of using masks. (*Brand*, no. 5, 1996)

A bridge resistance camp was organised by the action group, Social Ecological Action Malmö/Lund, from 20 June to 20 July 1996 which assembled activists from a wide range of various action groups. In addition to strategy discussions and actions against the bridge project, the camp was host to concerts, theatre, juggling workshops, courses in civil disobedience and self-defence, and lectures. (*Brand*, no. 5, 1996)

While road protesters and bridge protesters have concentrated their efforts to Stockholm and the bridge link between Malmö and Copenhagen, feminists throughout Sweden are stepping up their struggle. A temporary feminist action group in Lund spray-painted Hennes & Mauritz billboards in downtown Lund during the night of 16 November 1995 with the words: 'say no!'. The group protested against the exploitation of women in the department store's advertising. (*Brand* no. 1, 1996) Earlier in the month, the action group, 'Pippi Long-Stockings and her Militant Sisters and Brothers', marched through Stockholm one night spray-painting, smashing windows, and smearing excrement over ten pornoshops. While they were at it, they trashed a Shell station the same night. (Ibid.)

During the Christmas vacation in 1995, feminist action groups in Stockholm carried out a series of attacks, spray painting and window

smashing pornoshops in the city. Even the department store, Hennes
& Mauritz, had three large shop windows smashed as a protest against
their Christmas advertising campaign. The action group, 'A Porno
Free South Stockholm', carried out their action 'shit bomb' against the
premises of a pornographic video firm. (Ibid.) The Left Youth
Association, AFA (Antifascist Action) and SUF (the Syndicalism Youth
Association) arranged a 'picnic' in March, 1996 outside of the largest
pornographic video firm in Västerås. About 30 activists assembled
and jeered at the store's customers until the owner called for the police
to evacuate them from his property. No arrests were made. (*Brand,* no.
5, 1996) In May 1996 a video pornoshop was attacked with bricks,
iron bars and butyric acid, by the action group 'Anti-Sexist Hooligans'.
(*Brand,* no. 3, 1996)

Militant left action groups are broadening their adversarial front in
Sweden. It is difficult to pinpoint a centre of resistance in that they are
engaged in a cacophonous symphony of confrontation with points of
resistance they are creatively defining. For example, Third World
solidarity actions are being fought in Sweden bringing the political
struggle of the global periphery to a site in the centre. During the
night of 23 October 1995 an action group, 'some anti-imperialists',
attacked the premises in Lund of the multi-national company L. M.
Ericsson with molotov cocktails in protest against the company's sales
of the AXE electronic surveillance system to military dictatorships, both
domestic and foreign sales of weapons, Ericsson's involvement in the
Öresund bridge project, and a general protest against the company's
exploitation of the Third World. They released the following statement:

[w]e are sick and tired of Swedish companies that act like pigs around the
world without critique. Therefore our action is a reminder that we live in
imperialism's backyard. (*Brand* no. 1, 1996)

The action group, 'Sabotage for Communism', this time in Göteborg,
carried out another night-time attack with paint bombs against L. M.
Ericsson's premises. They connected their action to the previous action
in Lund and released the following statement: "[t]he struggle for
liberation is international! Shake imperialism at its centre! For socialism
and revolution!" (Ibid.) In the spring of 1996, the action group,
'Commando S. Pig', burned down the research facilities of L. M.
Ericsson in Lund in protest against the company's activities in the Third
World. In their press statement they stated:

[w]hile symbolic actions can be commendable, in this action we will cause direct economic damage. (The economic losses for Ericsson were estimated to exceed 15 million crones.) Our ambition was even to sabotage Ericsson's research activities ... we hoped to even make actual the anti-imperialist perspective within the militant resistance community in Sweden. We hope that our action will encourage militant action groups against sexism, anti-fascist groups, environmental groups and peace groups to include anti-imperialism in their struggle. (*Brand*, no. 3, 1996)

The multi-national petroleum company Shell has been the target of left-wing militant direct actions throughout the 1990s. For example, during February 1996 the action group, 'Ecological Action, Earth First Umeå!' carried out a number of actions against Shell stations in the community. On 8 February around 50 activists trashed a station for an estimated total damage of 15,000 crones. Later in the month the group trashed two other Shell stations, this time for an estimated 1,500,000 in damages and a 300,000 crones loss in sales. During the entire month, the group has spread flyers throughout the city with the message that "Shell's business in Nigeria is both ecologically repugnant and repulsive to human rights!". In general they claim that Shell actively supports the violence and human rights indignities carried out by military dictatorships throughout the world. (*Brand*, no. 2, 1996) During the month of April, the Action Group 'Boycott Shell', carried out a series of symbolic actions against Shell stations in the vicinity of Gävle in protest against the company's activities in Nigeria. They raised a Shell flag with skull and crossbones at one station, and at another they hung up a doll symbolising the executed human rights activist, Ken Sarowiva. Their goal was to awaken the attention of motorists to Shell's foreign involvement in military dictatorships. (*Brand*, no. 3, 1996) May, 1996 an action from the Västerås division of AFA calling themselves, 'AIZ-AO' (Anti-Imerialistiche Zelle/Ausland Organisation) burned a Shell station to the ground. (*Brand*, no. 3, 1996)

The McDonalds premises in Varberg were trashed in April 1996 by the local AFA group in protest against the multi-national franchise McDonalds' exploitation of the youth working force. In their press statement they encouraged others to boycott McDonalds and to carry out direct actions against the "multi-national vultures". (*Brand*, no. 3, 1996)

Adversaries are being found in more unlikely sites than multi-national companies. An action group formed in 1996, 'Fundamentalism Opposition', actively challenged the Swedish State Church's 'Easter

Offensive' by throwing symbolic red paint on their billboards. The group spread posters across the country with the messages: "God is Evil, Lucky for Us that He Doesn't Exist" and "No Gods, No Masters. Refuse to Bend Your Knees!". (*Brand*, no. 5, 1996) In 1997 an action group plowed up the green on the 18th hole at a golf course in southern Sweden in protest against the use of insecticides and artificial fertilisers.

Throughout the 1990s antiracist action groups and racist/fascist groups and organisations have clashed in ritualised confrontations. (Peterson, 1997a) For example, in March 1996 the antiracist action group, 'Birkastadens Antifa', trashed the shop premises of an outlet for nazi propaganda and paraphernalia. In their press release they stated that they refuse to tolerate the existence of fascist elements in their community. Furthermore, they stated that they choose to use violent methods because it is useless to meet them with silence. "It is even useless to just confront them with ideological arguments. Physical resistance is necessary!" In their press statement they promised to continue their violent actions as long as the shop remained a nazi meeting place.

In May 1996 another antiracist action group, 'Vasastans Antifa', carried out an arson attack against the same premises. In their press release they stated that their use of fire was controlled and a conscious strategy on their part. They emphasised that the operation was carried out in a way which would not jeopardise other occupants in the building and that this time, their goal, was not to injure any fascists on the premises. "Instead the goal was to show our resolution in the struggle". (*Brand*, no. 3, 1996)

This brief survey over examples of the actions of high-risk militant groups and action networks reveals the diversity of political discourses and practices they are intervening in, hence the diversity of their sites of resistance; they are creatively constructing their adversaries in an ongoing construction of the political terrain of action. Furthermore, the survey emphasises the manifold diversity and hybridisation of their action forms, which include both illegal violent forms of protest as well as legal forms of non-violent symbolic resistance.

The question of violence — other-directed, self-directed and/or property-directed, which is anticipated, threatened, or actual — is a distinguishing characteristic for the action repertoire of militant high-risk action groups. They are *per definition* militant high-risk action groups on the basis of their acceptance of violence in some form in their action tactics, in contrast with social movement groups and organisations which condemn the use of violence and advocate strictly non-violent procedures.[4] Addressing the issue of violent direct actions, as always a bone of contention within the wider social movement struggle, the editorial committee of *Brand* writes in a critique of the latest 'official' anti-violence campaign that violence can be directed upwards or downwards in the social hierarchy. According to the editors, when violence is directed downwards — against women, immigrants, young people, and homosexuals — it is a question of repression, in other words, the act of violence maintains existing social structures. When violence is directed upward, either as a conscious political action or as an apparently unpolitical action, it is a question of resistance. And subsequently, the editors argue it is in the interest of the state and the dominant classes to limit violence in society. According to the editors, if violence threatens to spread so as to pose a threat to the general public there is a risk that people begin to doubt the ability of the state to provide them with security. Hence, the state must confront the violence that fundamentally threatens its existence:

> with repression, naturally. More money to the police, new 'anti-terrorist' police, harder prison sentences. And with campaigns against 'others' violence. These anti-violence campaigns do not deal with pacifism in general, instead they deal with strengthening the monopoly of violence — the state's and the 'forces of good's' violence. But do these 'forces of good' call for anti-violence when the police batter demonstrators or immigrants? They don't demand stricter measures against men who beat or rape women. If these campaigns were really serious about coming to grips with violence in society then it would mean that white, middle-class, male, Swedish, in other words, the men behind these campaigns, would renounce their privileged monopoly over the means of violence. (*Brand*, no. 2, 1996)

In their critique of the state initiated anti-violence campaign these commentators argue for wresting the monopoly over the means of

---

4 Violent enactments of militant political protest is understood here, and throughout the book, in a broad sense. Militant left-wing groups more often assume Gandhian principles of non-violent action and civil disobedience and tend to shy away from enactments of other-directed violence, with some exceptions. Nevertheless, these action groups and networks all to various degrees employ self-directed and/or property-directed violent enactments. (see chapter three)

violence from the state and the utilisation of violent means in acts of resistance. They attempt to legitimise the use of violence in struggles by, and for, 'underdogs'. This issue divides even militant action groups. An ongoing discussion on the 'vegan' Internet homepage deals with the question of violence in the struggle. Per claims that while he understands the use of violence to save the weak, he argues that the use of violence to save a few animal lives is tactically wrong as the media then represents the vegan movement in negative terms which in turn results in fewer converts to their ideology and praxis, hence, in the long run, more animals suffer. Furthermore, Per argues that "violence breeds violence". Lisa argues against the deployment of violence in their struggle on similar grounds:

> There are great risks in using violence as a means to achieve a goal. The risks involved are directly connected with what violence begets for expectations. A positive development cannot be created with the use of violence as a means in large doses. Violence tends to augment fear, aggressiveness, revenge, etc., which take on a life of their own even after the original goals have been achieved. Violence as oppression and violence that liberates from oppression: there is no difference between the two forms for violence!

Claus counters these arguments in the following words:

> I see violence as necessary in order to defend the weak. Those who are not prepared to struggle for the weak with all necessary means are villains. However, the struggle can be pursued with different methods. For my part, I seldom employ violence. Most often I talk to people and show them that it is possible to live as a vegan through my own example. And I do not say that violence is justified or effective in every situation. However, we must not be afraid to use violence as a method to change the world or defend the victims of oppression. I object to all of the myths surrounding the use of violence such as 'violence breeds violence' and 'we can not use the same means as our dumb opponents'. I believe that frustration breeds violence. We must defend ourselves and those rights we have achieved. We must save those lives that otherwise would be lost. Anyone who says differently is either crazy or the enemy. Who benefits by our fuss over whether violence is justified or not? Go out and smash something instead!

Claus is both sceptical to the mass media and strategies that award priority to the struggle's 'media image'. "You can't trust the media or propaganda to change public opinion." Furthermore, he argues that he does not employ violence in order to change public opinion:

> I don't believe that people change if you crack them on the head. I use violence in order to damage my adversaries so that they cannot attack us, in order to break them.

What we have experienced in Sweden during the 1990s is the increased utilisation of violent action tactics on the part of militant left-wing high-risk groups and action networks, particularly the escalation of violence in the animal rights struggle in Sweden has led to a society-wide debate in the media. The rapid rise of a militant branch of the animal rights movement in Sweden during the 1990s has captured the attention of the Swedish people. Animal rights activists have waged a 'war' on behalf of animals across the country. Mink have been released in the tens of thousands, furrier shops have been attacked, research facilities have been entered, even bombed, and laboratory animals released, meat packer trucks have been bombed, veterinarians and researchers have been threatened. 'Vegan' youth have become, to the public eye, synonymous with masked militants. In the general 'moral panic' generated by these attacks, charges of terrorism and epitaphs of 'saboteurs' abound.

From 'Ideological Sects' to 'Action Sects'

The organised opposition to the war in Vietnam mobilised left wing youth in Sweden from 1966 to its final end in 1975. On the one hand, a 'New Left' emerged on the political scene with its emphasis upon direct action. Within the 'New Left' there was a strong scepticism against state authorities, political leadership in general, and bureaucracy in particular. Emphasis was placed upon spontaneity and individual political participation:

> People could achieve increased control over their own lives through participation in political activity. The 'New Left's' vision of a new society included the belief in the individual's capacity to participate in vital decisions which influenced his/her life. (Salomon, 1996: 75)

On the other hand, orthodox left-wing rhetoric were re-introduced and re-instated within the political left during the 1960s. FNL, the Swedish Anti-Vietnam War Movement, shortly after its emergence became dominated by a new left-wing party which was founded in 1967, the Communist Marxist-Leninist Association (KFML). KFML had as its principle political goal to transform Swedish society in a revolutionary direction. In short, a humanitarian anti-war movement was itself transformed back to the classical rhetoric of class struggle. The concept of anti-imperialism became the all-embracing doctrine behind the anti-war rhetoric of the FNL movement in Sweden, and it was this doctrine which was to serve as the political link between an opposition to American involvement in a war across the globe and the domestic class struggle. A central committee for the locally based anti-war groups across the country was established, the United FNL Groups (DFFG), first as an umbrella organisation to act as co-ordinator and information channel between the groups and later as a central association with its own political programme. With KFML's 'take-over' of the central leadership within the DFFG, the organisational strategy adopted, so-called 'democratic centralism', effectively smothered dissident voices and spontaneous actions within the fledgling movement. Incorporating Leninism's elitist strategies, KFML saw itself as a political avante guarde, which would ignite the spark of revolution within Swedish society, mobilised on a broad popular front against the war in Vietnam. Subsequently, FNL was seen as a recruitment base for the new revolutionary party in Sweden. It was this side of the widespread youth mobilisation against the war in Vietnam that was to emerge victorious. The 'New Left', with its questioning of traditional left-wing doctrines and its aim to re-vitalise democratic organisational forms, was effectively outmanoeuvered by the more orthodox left wing. The Anti-Vietnam Movement, the FNL, sprang forth in the intersection between the old and the new, between the popular movements or folk movements of the past and the 'new social movements' of the future. The wider Anti-Vietnam Movement was, on the one side, closely allied with the established folk movement culture of the unions, religious organisations and party-political youth associations and of the Social Democratic Swedish Committee for Vietnam, which posed the strongest governmental critique of USA involvement in the war in the western world; and on the other side, the anti-establishment mobilisation of young people's engagement manifested in the FNL movement, which paradoxically constructed its identity in the struggle with its strong opposition to the Social Democratic Party and its government, and its unquestioned allegiance to the traditional orthodoxy of communist doctrines. At this historical intersection both sides of the Swedish Anti-War movement (FNL), both its establishment wing and its anti-establishment wing, allied themselves with the past, even if the seeds of the new which were sown at this time. The streets as a political arena — would later bloom forth in the 'new' social movement terrain of the latter 1970s.

If the Swedish FNL movement's ideological praxis could be summarised by the slogans: 'combat USA imperialism' and 'USA out of Vietnam', so could the FNL movement's political praxis be summarised with the concepts of 'focal point' and 'united front'. (Cf. Solomon, 1996) Focal point theory claimed that USA imperialism could only be combated one step at a time, therefore forces in the struggle should be concentrated to that area where USA imperialism was at its weakest point, which according to FNL leadership in Sweden, was Vietnam. Subsequently, the movement was reluctant to disperse their energies to engagements in other international conflicts, such as the question of Palestine, apartheid in South Africa, and the overthrow of the socialist Chilean regime in 1973. Furthermore, as KFML's political strategy was focused upon the struggle against 'USA imperialism in Vietnam', this left-wing group even felt distracted by the wave of wildcat strikes which broke out in Sweden during the latter 1960s. The key to their interpretation of the transformation of Swedish society to a revolutionary society was the struggle against USA imperialism in Vietnam, so even the domestic struggles, which broke out in the mining districts of northern Sweden, were translated into USA imperialism rhetoric. (Cf. Soloman, 1996) In short, 'focal point' strategy emphasised the necessity of concentrating the struggle to one single issue deemed central to the overall goals of radical struggle. 'Focal point' strategy which dominated the radical wing of the anti-Vietnam movement during this period finds little resonance in the militant struggles of the 1990s which is characterised rather by its wide diversification of political issues and sites for political resistance.

The latter strategy, 'united front', had as its aim to broaden the political struggle to include even non-socialist sympathisers. The underlying aim was to mobilise on a broad front first, and afterhand to socialise the participants in its ideology. It was thought that an emotional engagement and spontaneity could be later harnessed by 'political correctness'. The united front strategy had its historical roots in the popular front ideas from the 1930s when left-wing organisations and groups, from radical socialists to communists, united themselves in a popular front to ward off the threats posed by fascist parties in Sweden at that time. Furthermore, FNL's united front strategy was influenced by Mao Zedung's thinking from the same historical period when he developed the popular front strategy in connection with China's struggle against the Japanese invasion in the latter 1930s. Mao and Mao's 'little red book' became increasingly the most influential political inspiration for the Swedish FNL movement.

The united front strategy which emphasised a development from confrontation politics to co-operation with its toned down rhetoric, 'softer ideology', and openness to co-operation in the struggle across the political spectrum, opened up as well to the internal struggles within the left in Sweden. Confrontation politics became an internal affair for the radical left in Sweden, consolidated at that time in the FNL movement. First, with the so-called 'rebel movement' from 1968, a radical wing of Maoists (even called 'red guardists' and 'liquidators') and later with KFML's schism and eventual split in 1973 which led to the formation of KFMLr, the Communist Association of Marxist-Leninist Revolutionaries, and SKP, the Swedish Communist Party, which retained its Maoist political doctrines. (Salomen, 1996) The Swedish political map blossomed with a flora of new alphabetical constellations on the left: VPK (the parliamentary communist party, Left Party Communists), APK, SKP, KFMLr, and SP. In short, what developed was a flora of 'ideological sects', literally faithful to its own particular doctrine derived from interpretations of Marxist-Leninism, Stalinism, Maoism, and the 'third international' of Trotskyism. Small, ideologically exclusive, radical left-wing groups more and more fought a bitter and emotionally charged struggle between themselves — over words, and through words. Radicalism was expressed by 'talk'. The cadre ideological discipline, which distinguished this generation of Swedish radicals, finds little appeal among the new generation of militants that emerged in Sweden in the 1990s. The 'action sects' of the 1990s are a far cry from the 'ideological sects' of the 1970s.

Thirdly, the organisational strategy of 'democratic centralism' which dictated the organisational structure of FNL finds literally no resonance in the organisational strategies of militant politics during the 1990s. The notion of a revolutionary sophisticated leadership, which would educate and socialise its grassroots sympathisers into a 'correct' ideological interpretation of its doctrines, is foreign to the grassroots democratic autonomy of contemporary militant politics.

While, for example, FNL's romantic view of the revolutionary potential of the working class and its emphasis upon the education of 'propagandists' to spread its message to the uninformed, as well as its door-to-door campaigning, appear somewhat out of date today, many of the characteristics of political militancy from the FNL era live on today in Sweden. The 'demonstration culture' which was rejuvenated in the 1960s with FNL's symbolic demonstrations and police confrontations, its acts of violent civil disobedience which, however, were restrained to throwing eggs at representatives for the United States in Sweden and the detonation of a smoke bomb in the cinema showing the film, 'The Green Berets' (11 pople were hospitalised for smoke inhalation, but the distribution of the film in Sweden was stopped), its mass media orientation and construction of its own alternative media channels, primarily its production and distribution of *Vietnam Bulletin*, which reached a sales of over 60,000 in the spring months of 1972, are all militant strategies which resonate with contemporary militant politics. Perhaps the most intimate relationship with the FNL movement shared by today's political militants can be summarised as 'political activism as a lifestyle'. Today's militant youth like yesterday's FNL activists devote whole-heartedly their lives to their cause — their everyday lives are emersed in their political struggle. Political militancy is a way of life. However, in summarising in the pages above the three primary contrasting characteristics of radical politics in the era of FNL from 1968-1975 with the militant movements of the 1990s one can say that the 'old' has been left farther behind in favour of the 'new left' politics of grassroots democracy, individual political responsibility, the strategy of direct action, and the spontaneity of emotional engagement and moral protest which found its dominant position in the political map which developed after the Anti-Vietnam Movement in Sweden with the appearance of the women's liberation movement, the environmental movement, and the peace movement in the latter 1970s and 1980s. Militant politics today, while they of course bear the marks of their historical predecessors from the 1960s and 1970s, if nothing else in the form of their organisational exclusivity or sectarianism and the subjugation of their private everyday lives to their political struggle, can be perceived as a further radicalisation of the 'new social movement' politics which directly proceeded them. Contemporary militant politics are emotionally charged, moral protests against a wide range of perceived social injustices where actions are given priority over words — its what you do, not what you say, that makes today's politics radical and activists militant.

Lastly, if international conflicts such as the war in Vietnam, apartheid in South Africa, the questions of Palestine, and liberation movements across the globe in general, engaged earlier generations of radical youth, international politics today have moved home to us here in Sweden. Since the latter 1960s the ethnic map of Sweden has become fundamentally transformed and these changes are permanent. Sweden, in a few short decades, has become a multicultural society. Questions of international solidarity which once engaged our youth have become increasingly questions of domestic solidarity with Swedes with immigrant and refugee backgrounds — the so-called 'new' Swedes. And perhaps the single ideological common denominator embraced by contemporary youth militants on the far-left in Sweden is antiracism, while on the far-right youth militancy is united by its racist and nationalist politics.

The Durkheimian Notion of Political Ritual

Rituals are a ubiquitous part of modern political life. Through participation in political rites, for example the football crowd belting out the national anthem, the citizen of the modern state identifies with larger political forces that can only be seen in symbolic form. Through political rituals individuals experience a sense of 'we', of solidarity, with a political abstract 'whole', whether that 'whole' is a nation, a global community, an ethnic community, a social movement struggle, or a specific militant action group. Rituals weld together political collectives, large and small. (Cf. Lukes, 1975) Participation in political rites may encourage and maintain the status quo by mystifying relations of power, providing legitimacy, and disguising internal conflicts — an aspect of consensus construction which is most often emphasised in the theorising regarding political ritual. Even the counter-hegemonic political communities we are discussing here rely upon ritual to cement the bonds that connect individual participants. So aside from their intended effects upon the political system in that these action networks or groups are challenging existing power relations, they have an internal interest in the maintenance of the hegemonic character of the militant action network/group itself. Subsequently, political ritual will be discussed here as the function and form of political action, which coalesces the militant action network/group, which constructs a sense of 'we', their sense of group solidarity.

However, political rituals may actualise a set of symbols that challenge existing structures of power, revealing inequities and bringing to the surface underlying conflicts, thereby carving out new bases for political solidarity. In this latter sense, political rituals are valuable instruments for struggles of resistance. For example, militant high-risk action groups, in that they are at odds with the dominant political culture, perhaps rely even to a greater degree upon political ritual as a source for their collective identity construction, their sense of group solidarity, but they are even committed to challenging the status quo of what they perceive as the wider social movement within which they are a part, as well as society at large.   Esherick and Wasserstrom (1990) make a valuable analytical distinction between two genres of public political performances: that between "political ritual" and "political theatre". According to these theorists, political rituals serve to "support and reinforce the status quo, bringing order to a community" (of any size) "by reaffirming the distinctions between and bonds connecting its individual members". (p. 844) Political rituals do so by careful adherence to a traditionally prescribed script of political action. Political theatre, on the other hand, departs from this traditional script of action, and in so doing, challenges the status quo. People can, and do, turn ritual performances into acts of political theatre. They agree that this distinction is heuretical, that the line of demarcation between the two genres of action is unclear, and that a grey area exists wherein ritual and theatre overlap. Furthermore, political ritual involves ritual processes that are unstable or liminal, and which are open for people to subvert to other ends, what will be described in the next chapter as hijacking the ritual event.

So indeed, far from simply propping up the status quo of society in general, political ritual, potentially political theatre, is used to make claims to power and to send messages to the public; here in the sense that militant activists turn a ritual performance into an act of political theatre.

Meaning is embedded in ritual actions. Political rites encourage certain interpretations of the world. They do so in no small part because of the powerful emotions that they trigger. The common denominator among political rituals in general is their manufacture of an emotionally charged rendition of reality between a 'we' and 'them', between 'forces of good' and 'forces of evil'. (Peterson, 1997a) The ritual performance is primarily designed to impress and 'move' an audience emotionally; it is not a lecture to inform. These 'we/them' distinctions are most vividly experienced and emotionally compelling in ritual confrontations with movement adversaries. Violence, or simply the potential for violence, in ritual confrontations by the militant high-risk action groups we are analysing, enacts and re-enacts this theme of 'we' contra 'them', thereby cementing both sides in the struggle. Violence is a bearer of meaning for these groups. The emotions of embattlement render the cognitive message of the ritual — 'forces of good in a righteous struggle with the forces of evil' — compelling. Emotions generate meaning and actions become meaningful through the lived/living experiences of ritual confrontation. How can the messages of militant action groups be contested when they are framed by the ritual confrontations that bring violence (or the potential of) onto the bodies of the participants? The emotional dramas of ritual confrontations, utilising violence or the potential of violence — other-directed, self-directed and/or directed towards property — bear the lived/living meanings of the actions for their participants.

Politics is expressed through symbolism. In order to understand the political processes of militant action, then it is necessary to understand how the symbolic enters into their politics. It is argued here that ritual confrontation (more precisely designated as political theatre) is one important vehicle for how the symbolic enters militant politics. Ritual confrontation is a symbolically constructed rite of violence (self-, other-, and/or property-directed), or potential violence, with their adversary(ies). Violence bears the meaning of the ritual event of confrontation. Ritual in this sense is a reflectively constructed enactment of violence against a reflectively constructed adversary(ies). The underlying narrative of ritual confrontation is the construction of collective identities, their emotionally charged sense of interdependence in the drama they enact — an interdependence upon their fellow participants in their respective militant groups and/or the riot squads called to 'police' them; an interdependence upon the existence of their adversaries in the drama of the ritual confrontation, these groups, as well as the police, mutually award meaning to each other in the confrontation. These ritual confrontations construct the collective identities, their senses of solidarity, for all of the protagonists in the drama. They do so through the emotions they unleash. The ritual of confrontation is wrapped in a web of violent symbolism that engulfs the participants in an emotionally charged sense of solidarity and common purpose, affirming and reaffirming their collective political identities.

The sociologist who first recognised the ubiquity of political ritual, and who remains one of its most powerful theorists, is Émile Durkheim.

Émile Durkheim and the 'Magical Moment' of Political Ritual

Few sociologists and political scientists have recognised how important ritual is in modern politics. Rituals are usually identified with religion; hence the assumption has persisted that ritual remains politically significant only in less 'advanced' or 'primitive' societies. For example, British historian Eric Hobsbawn (1959) in his book *Primitive Rebels* argues that the importance of ritual for labour organisations can be traced back to a pre-industrial residue and the importance of ritual for the labour movement subsequently diminishes with the advent of modernism. The study of rituals and political life has been largely left *de facto* to anthropologists.

According to Charles Lindholm (1990), Durkheim was ostensibly inspired by ethnographies of so-called 'primitive' cultures for his understanding of ritual and collective effervescence, however, in the back of his mind was the French Revolution which he referred to as the prototypical example of a depersonalising and invigorating ritual in the modern era:

> The Revolution demonstrates, he [Durkheim] tells us, that the emotional essence of religion is not related to gods or creeds, but rises out of spontaneous mass celebrations and the collective passions these generate. (Lindholm, 1990: 30)

Or in Durkheim's (1965) own words:

> [t]his aptitude of society for setting itself up as a god or for creating gods was never more apparent than during the first years of the French Revolution. At this time, in fact, under the influence of the general enthusiasm,

things purely laic by nature were transformed by public opinion into sacred things: these were the Fatherland, Liberty, and Reason. . I t is true that this religious renovation had only an ephemeral duration. But that was because the patriotic enthusiasm which at first transported the masses soon relaxed. ... But this experiment, though short-lived, keeps all its sociological interest. It remains true that in one determined case we have seen society and its essential ideas become, directly and with no transfiguration of any sort, the object of a veritable cult. (p. 214)

So while Durkheim relied heavily upon empirical sources from so called 'primitive societies', particularly from ethnographies of Aboriginal peoples, his theorising over the role of ritual was intended in more general terms. His choice of empirical materials was motivated rather by what he regarded as the 'pure' forms expressed by rituals in these more 'primitive' contexts; what is more readily accessible in the rites of 'primitive' peoples, was more obtuse in the rites among his contemporaries.

In the work of Durkheim collective effervescence is the process whereby individuals transcend themselves to the higher order of the group. The creative principle is shared participation in highly charged and depersonalising rituals of the sacred which serve to integrate all of the members into a unit. Durkheim's contribution to the widespread observations of the equalising and energising experience of collective action was his explanation as to its source and shape in the 'moment of communion'. According to Durkheim (1965), emotional effusions of selflessness are engendered automatically whenever people are put "into closer and more active relations with one another". (p. 241) When a certain density of people gathers, the actual physical intimacy and propinquity of the crowd inevitably obliges people to feel a sense of sharing:

The similarity of the crowd members is accentuated by their physical closeness; they begin to feel their individual identities disintegrating under the influence of the crowd massed around them. Under these circumstances Durkheim thought that collective effervescence is bound to occur regardless of any cultural differences since the fundamental process is always the same; only circumstances colour it differently. (Lindholm, 1990: 30)

It is not just physical proximity and intimacy which brings forth collective effervescence, it is also inspired by spontaneous emotional outbursts which are contagiously spread and imitated, magnified, and synchronised within the group as a whole. Collective effervescence, as defined by Durkheim, is an automatically induced experience of exaltation and self-loss. However, Durkheim modifies this position by maintaining that the process can be induced consciously though the manufacture of symbolic forms — charismatic leaders, chants, gestures, songs, etc. — which can serve as foci for the vivifying collective ritual. In fact, in order that a state of collective effervescence can survive beyond the 'moment of communion' the group must revivify their collective experiences with periodical reunions. Durkheim (1965) argues that:

> to strengthen those sentiments which, if left to themselves, would soon weaken, it is sufficient to bring those who hold them together and to put them into closer and more active relations with one another. (p. 210)

Hetherington (1998) argues that too much of the work in the past (i.e. primarily Durkheim and his followers) focused on the charismatic leader and not upon the elective conditions that lie as the source of the charismatic community. He claims that:

> a generalisation of charisma within groups seeking to disperse this 'substance' in the form of 'energy' or 'commitment' to all members of the Bund will probably be favoured over charismatic leaders. Charisma in this general sense is likely to be perceived as the basis of authentic, unmediated interpersonal relationships, expressed through the performativity of the occasion as well as within a Bund rather than through the adoration of a leader. Such empathic relations come to be seen as unmediated and direct, based purely in feeling. (pp. 93-94)

Rituals constitute, enact, and reproduce the very forces they represent and therefore give persons who participate in them the experience of necessary force. Through the ritual event, the members of the assembled group 'make it' and 'remake it' as a moral community. Practices that enact moral relationships produce 'feelings' of moral force. And together with the event of the ritual, an image may even act profoundly upon the community in linking its members. This might be a conventional emblem or symbol, a sign that is in principle banal, but which on the occasion of a particular rite becomes a totem, an "image of a sacred thing". These images, for example, a flag or even an ordinary word, can achieve the function of a sign and become a means of recognition or serve as a rallying cry. In each of these cases, an image reinforces the social ties within the community that thereby once again finds its "original vigour". Jamison and Eyerman (1997), also following Durkheim's lead, point out the potential of music for transmitting this emotional energy or commitment, what Hetherington calls the generalisation of charisma.

But to return to Durkheim, the collective effervescence generated by the enacted practices of rituals is the very stuff of the social. Rituals unleash powerful emotions that are the substance of group solidarity. Through the process of collective effervescence — the magical moment of group fusion — individuals are strengthened and expanded, feeling themselves as part of something larger and more powerful than themselves. Collective effervescence is the practical result of concrete social practices. The feeling of moral unity is the purpose of the ritual. And it is not in the mind nor is this sense of community added by the mind. Solidarity is achieved through individuals acting together, not by people thinking together. Furthermore, the feeling of moral unity, or sense of community, is the substance of the enacted practices of ritual and therefore external, general and shared, not internal and individual. The assembled participants in the processes of collective effervescence inherent in the ritual are lifted 'above and beyond' themselves.

For Durkheim ritual is a means by which we express our social dependence. What is important in ritual is our common participation and emotional involvement, not the specific rationalisations by which we account for the rite. Hence, rites are not simply stylised statements of belief or ideology. It is the form of the ritual that matters and through which its underlying discursive force is carried, not its content. Indeed participants in the same ritual may, and often do, attribute different meanings to their participation. The strength of Durkheim's analysis lies in his recognition that ritual constructs solidarity, and does not necessarily require the sharing of beliefs. It is in people acting together, not in people thinking together, that group solidarity is generated.

Rituals have been a favourite object of study among anthropologists, however, rituals are not the exclusive property of group life in far away places among so-called primitive peoples. Rituals are just as much a part of group life in contemporary complex societies. Politics and political life in general, would indeed be barren without political rituals that reinforce and create political communities, large and small. Politics is expressed through symbolism and the symbolic enters into politics through rituals. Political actors, the state as well as militant political groups or the political neo-sects under investigation here, all consciously manipulate symbols, constructing in turn rituals. David Kertzer (1988) has defined ritual as action wrapped in a web of symbolism where symbolisation gives the action its meanings. (Cf. Esherick and Wasserstrom, 1990; Lukes, 1975; and Swartz, 1985) Through the enacted practices of rituals, beliefs about the action environment come to be acquired, reinforced, and eventually changed. Most analysts of rituals have focused upon how ritual is employed to conserve political systems by fulfilling important organisational needs, by providing legitimacy at the same time as it mystifies actual power relations, by facilitating popular solidarity even when consensus is conspicuously absent, and by leading people to conceive of their political universe in certain ways. However, Kertzer points out that in many respects ritual is even more important for revolutionary groups than it is to long-established political organisations or regimes. For the same reasons that ritual is important to all political organisations for the maintenance of political consensus, ritual is vital to the militant neo-sect if they are to incite political conflict and disrupt the prevailing norms of politics. The neo-sect's exclusivity and political commitment is contingent upon the bonds of solidarity that cement the activists together. It is through emotionally shared rituals that these bonds of solidarity are achieved and the politics of 'disorder' are subsumed to ordering processes of collective identity construction.

Collective Representations or the 'Metaphysical Product'

What we have hitherto discussed is the process, and the constituent elements within this process — emotional intensity, rituals and rites, symbols — that imbue a sense of 'we-ness' or collective belonging. Now, if we take the discussion one step further in the sociology of Durkheim, we come to Durkheim's notion of collective representation. According to Durkheim, the organisation of the crowd or affectual group is only finally effected when the attention of the individuals who compose it becomes focussed upon some particular object or some particular objective. This object thus fixed in the focus of the attention of the group tends to assume the character of a collective representation. It becomes this because it is the focus of the collectively enhanced emotion and sentiment of the group. It becomes the representation and the symbol of what the group feels and wills at the moment when all members are suffused with a common collective excitement and dominated by a common collective idea. This excitement, and this idea with the meanings that attach to it, is called collective because it is a product of the interactions of the members of the crowd. They are not individual but corporate products. (See Durkheim, 1965, pp. 432-437)

Durkheim defines collective representations as the concepts that embody the objectives of group activity:

> The totem of primitive peoples, the flag of a nation, a religious creed, the number system, and Darwin's theory of the descent of man — all these are collective representations. (Ibid. 436)

Every society and every social group has, or tends to have, its own symbols and its own language. The language and other symbolic devices by which a society carries on its collective existence are collective representations. And it is through the *enacted practices* of collective representations that a community, a social group, or indeed, society as a whole, is embued with collective consciousness or sense of moral force. Collective consciousness:

> being placed outside of and above individual and local contingencies, it sees things only in their permanent and essential aspects, which it crystallises into communicable ideas. At the same time that it sees from above, it sees farther; at every moment of time, it embraces all known reality; that is why it alone can furnish the mind with the moulds which are applicable to the totality of things and which make it possible to think of them. It does not create these moulds artificially; it finds them within itself; it does nothing but become conscious of them .... With collective representations the germ of a new mentality was given, to which the individual could never have raised himself by his own efforts; by them the way was opened to a stable, impersonal and organised thought which then had nothing to do except to develop its nature. (Ibid. 437)

Maffesoli (1996b) argues that Durkheim's notion of collective consciousness is quite pertinent for understanding contemporary society and:

its various effervescences, which all are effected around, or on the basis
of, sentiments, emotions, images, symbols — causes and effects of this
collective consciousness. (p. 89)

Collective consciousness, as the notion is interpreted by Maffesoli,
is the impulse that links people together, what he calls, "that mysterious
cement — nonlogical, nonrational" — which is the basis of, the very
precondition for, the 'social'. The collective consciousness understood
as immaterial aura issues from society, returns toward it in order to
constitute and comfort social life. Collective consciousness, understood
in this sense, approaches what Durkheim called *social force*. Rawls (1996)
argues that Durkheim's socioempiricism focuses on the dynamic
relations between group members as participants in ritual social
processes and the social processes that their participation enacts:

Social forces are inherently dynamic and continuous and, when perceived
as such by persons assembled to enact practices, provide an empirical
source for the categories. (p. 433)

It was by means of these dynamics that Durkheim, according to
Rawls, was able to address the gap between thought and reality,
individual and group, that forms the basis of his social based
epistemology, and subsequently bypass the idealist position he has
been so tenaciously attributed.

From a discussion of the 'magical moment' of group construction,
collective effervescence, to a discussion of the magical and somewhat
metaphysical notion of collective representations and collective
consciousness, that is, the outcome of the intensive and emotional
interaction which constitutes the social in the sense of a feeling of
belonging, is not unproblematic. Durkheim's writing on collective
representations and collective consciousness bear a certain degree of
intangibility. While collective representations and collective
consciousness understood in the strict sense as enacted practices
informed by a Durkheimian socioempirical epistemology, disengages
an idealist interpretation, they have nevertheless readily lent
themselves to universal and essentialist (miss)interpretations by social
theorists insensitive to Durkheim's epistemology. For example, for
post-modern social theorists such as Stjepan Mestrovic (1991) and
Michael Maffesoli (1995, 1996a and 1996b) the Durkheimian notion of

collective representations is an invaluable tool in apprehending the import of religion (in its broadest and also 'secular' senses), as well as art and literature, within post-modernity. Collective representations symbolise or reflect underlying, objective social realities. They tell us something about the 'state' of society. For example, Mestrovic (1991) has followed Durkheim's lead in apprehending religion as a system of collective representations that betray something about the state of collective conscience of a particular society. Mestrovic argues that "as in psychoanalysis, society is the patient, and religious beliefs, rites, and symbols are the symptoms". (p. 160) These symptoms, according to Mestrovic, reveal post-modern society's deep-seated disenchantment with the world and rejection of rationalism. For Maffesoli, the "time of the tribes" is the ambience that the collective representations of contemporary neo-tribalism lend to post-modernity, its aura of "re-enchantment with the world". While connecting to Durkheim's notion of collective representations and interpreting the notion in idealist terms, undeniably allows these theorists to bypass what they perceive as the relativism and nihilism of much post-modern social theory, I would question whether the notion does not lend a metaphysical aura of reductionism to their sweeping statements as to the post-modern era's ambience (Maffesoli) or 'state' (Mestrovic). The question is perhaps not so much whether collective representation as sets of shared values and beliefs is an underlying precondition (both cause and effect) for social life, or whether religion (in either its sacred or secular forms) as a system of collective representations promotes social solidarity and strengthens the unity of the group, but whether one can indeed penetrate beneath them in order to reduce the complexity of contemporary sociality to universal and essential characteristics. I argue that both Maffesoli and Mestrovic, in their idealist misinterpretations of the Durkheimian notions of collective representation and collective consciousness, turn towards universal, underlying characteristics which are so highly mediated, in this case the collective, that while they become ontologically secure, they become 'emptied out' and 'abstract'. In particular Maffesoli, who celebrates the multiform, specific, cacophonous contemporary expressions of community, nevertheless, with this neglect of Durkheim's epistemology of enacted practices, falls victim to moral-political universals in his analysis, and this, despite his outspoken denial of normative judgements in his research. (Cf. Peterson, 1998)

Words or Deeds?

One critical point which underlies the work of modernity's early theorists, as well as connects them to the post-modern theorists discussed here, was the irrationality they assigned *per se* to the 'groupism' they observed which was based upon emotional and affective bonding. With the notable exceptions of Émile Durkheim and Georg Simmel,[5] they tended to more or less neglect the rationality of the actions of these groups, ignoring the creative dimensions of collective action within affective, intensely emotional groups. Even in less structured forms of collective action, people do not act in a void. They are always enmeshed in relations with other actors, express their needs, formulate meaning and activate their relationships within an action space. Political protests are always rational phenomena, understood not in a restricted normative sense, i.e. counterpoised with a notion of the rational as solely a means/end calculation, but as constituted through reflectively constructed collective actions. Protest actions are always socially constructed and are, subsequently, more or less meaningful for their participants. However, these early theorists, given the historical context of revolutionary upheaval, were confined within the pervading discourse or analytical foundation of their era which regarded all 'mass behaviour' or collective action as irrational, perceiving collective action as a form of social pathology which is produced by the disequilibrium within a social order. The discourse on the pathology of collective action continued to dominate the social sciences well into the 1960s with theorists such as Kornhauser (1959) and Smelser (1963), and today by theorists such as Mestrovic (1991).

Maffesoli (1996), while in contrast to Mestrovic, does not regard collective action in pathological terms, he does argue in terms of the underlying irrationalism of contemporary collective action. He maintains that passion and acts of passion are still the essential pivots around which social life revolves. Justifications, theorisation and rationalisations come *after* the event.

---

5 Georg Simmel (1950) stresses that the underlying characteristic of secret societies is their self-reflexive construction. According to Simmel, secret societies do not spring to life as an emotional outburst, rather they are rationally built. The rituals and hierarchical organization which characterize this *form of sociation*, are rationally constructed so as to *protect* their secrets, and hence their existence, and to maintain their *autonomy*, which is their essence. In chapter four I discuss secrecy as more or less a bonding principle of militant groups in terms of a rational organisation of emotions.

The primal element is the impulse to act and speak that presides over various aggregates, that encourages attraction and repulsion, and organises alliances, or in short all the 'non-logical' elements (Pareto) which we cannot ignore here and which are basic to our mode of being. According to Durkheim, for example, nearly every collective representation is in a sense delirious. (p. 60)

Both Maffesoli and Mestrovic are in different ways carrying on the legacy of modernity's early social theorists' preoccupation with the irrationality of collective action. Their analysis of contemporary collective action bears with it the notion of collective representations as a discursive reconstruction or rationalisation after the event. Subsequently, collective action is *per definition* irrational, and the emotions induced by the action can only be awarded meaning after the fact. On this point they are entering the hen and egg controversy in regards to collective representations or discourse. Durkheim's notion of collective representations and his related notion of collective consciousness bear with them a metaphysical aura and an idealist (miss) interpretation of his understanding on this point tends to strip collective action of its underlying meaning and logic for its participants. However, for Durkheim, collective representations, as meaningful systems of thought shared by corporate actors, are intrinsically interwoven in their collective actions.These collective actions and the passions aroused by collective rituals, i.e. collective effervescence — the 'magical moment' — can only be explained in pre-discursive or non-representational terms. Judith Butler (1997) offers an elegant path out of this Durkheimian *impasse* with her J. L. Austin inspired notion of the performative. Consider the following:

[t]he illocutionary speech act performs its deed *at the moment* of the utterance, and yet to the extent that the moment is ritualised, it is never merely a single moment. The 'moment' in ritual is a condensed historicity: it exceeds itself in past and future directions, an effect of prior and future invocations that constitute and escape the instance of utterance. (p. 3)

What Butler is eluding to appears to be a notion of the historicity of the present in which speech is an enacted practice, a form of social action. Through language, an "utterance", people do not primarily make a description *of* the world; they perform action *in* the world.

This historicity of the now, which exceeds in all directions of the history of the speaking/acting subject, bears resemblance to Søren Kierkegaards 'øyenblikk' and Walter Benjamin's *jetztzeit*, the messianic time of the 'now'. The now of enacted practices, implicated in a language whose historicity includes a past and present that "exceeds that of the subject who speaks" (Ibid. 28) is situated in the collective representations which they in turn effect. Hence, the 'magical moment' of collective effervescence is neither pre-discursive nor non-representational. Meaning is not awarded *after* the fact as in the case of irrational action, nor *before* the fact as in the case of rational action in which action is calculated to produce certain effects, but *during* the fact. For Durkheim, society consists of enacted practices, e.g. collective effervescences that give rise to real social forces that participants in the assembled group experience jointly and meaningfully. These enacted practices are not ideals. Collective representations are merely secondary phenomena (although embedded within) the fundamental 'magical moments' of sociality, that is, share enacted practices.

We can find here a justification for the dogma articulated by Ulkrike Meinhof, the *Rote Armé* activist in the early 1970s, that is, 'the supremacy of praxis'. This is an action dogma expressed time and again among the militant activists in our study. Put quite simply, they put 'deeds before words' claiming that "it always pays to resist". Their ideological work, while ongoing and indeed important to the group, is not primary. It is their ritual actions or political theatre that lend them their collective meanings. What Durkheim says is that ritual practices are the means by which social dependence is expressed and solidarity achieved. What is important for the group is their joint participation and emotional involvement, not the specific rationalisations, meanings, ideological messages by which they account for these ritual actions (indeed individual activists may very well lend different meanings to their ritual actions). (Cf. Peterson and Thörn, 1994) This would suggest that without discounting the discursive labour performed within these groups — the formulation of their truth claims — it is nevertheless the enacted practices of theatrical ritual confrontations which lend them their political force — *fatti maschii, parole femine.*[6]

---

6 While this familiar Latin quote is usually understood as meaning that 'deeds are more effective than words', literally translated it contains an interesting gender aspect. That is, 'deeds are males, words are females', hence, the 'natural' superiority of deeds over words.

Conclusion

In what ways can modernity's early theorists shed light upon the contemporary expressions of 'groupism', phenomena that I have designated as neo-sectarianism? Schmalenbach's reinterpretation of the concept of *Gemeinschaft* and his distinction between community and Bund are crucial for an understanding and conceptualisation of political groups which are elective and are held together primarily by emotional bonds of solidarity. In a sense the sociality of the *Bund* characterises the ambience of contemporary political struggle — both 'backstage' political activities interwoven in their everyday life practices and the overt 'frontstage' political theatre enacted in the streets and squares of our cities.

Central to the form of sociality of emotions is the notion of fusion, which is emphasised by Schmalenbach. *Fusion* is a process whereby individuals become imbedded within the group and a collective group identity emerges. Durkheim designated this process of fusion as *collective effervescence*. Collective effervescence, a moment of intense emotionality, is based upon shared lived/living experiences occurring during 'rare' moments or what Hetherington (1998), inspired by the work of Carl Schmitt, calls 'occasions'. I have emphasised in my research the importance of confrontation for the construction of what I have called neo-sects. Conflicts, or more precisely, ritualised physical confrontations, are those rare moments of emotional intensity which enhance processes of collective effervescence, therein lies the processes of group fusion. (Peterson, 1995 and Peterson, 1997a)

Durkheim formulated the core of what has become the most influential theory of social cohesion, emphasising the key role played by rituals, which generate emotional senses of solidarity or collective identity. People do not think together, they act together. The enacted practices of emotionally charged ritual confrontations lend the political neo-sect its collective identity and, in turn its political meaning(s). Political violence, whether this violence is other-, self- and/or property-directed, anticipated, threatened, and/or actual, is a genre of "emplotted" action (Feldman, 1991:14) or as understood here in Durkheimian terms, theatrical political ritual. An enactment of violence, the ritual confrontation, invests the bodies of the militant group with agency — the force with which the militant group intervenes in historicity.

The question posed here: 'how do various kinds of militant social movement groups create solidarity in order to further their political ends?' founds its basis of explanation in the work of Émile Durkheim. A reading of Durkheim's later body of work which is sensitive to his unique socioempirical epistemological position and which subsequently places into focus his notion of shared enacted practices (interaction) for the study of social, and hence, collective phenomena, lends us theoretical insights for our understanding of contemporary collective identity construction — the 'new explosive' forms of political community which are emerging in today's complex societies.

3 The Militant Body and Political Communication: The Medialisation of Violence

This chapter will not deal with the invisible, abstract body(ies) steering the disciplined bodies of the Hobbesian body politic, rather here we will analyse the visible, passionate bodies of militant political resistance — the ways in which the body 'embodies' political struggle, i.e. the ways in which the body is implicated in militant political resistance and political messages are 'bodied forth'. In the struggle against existing structures of power the body is the most primary interface of powers of resistance. However the body is more than an interface of the powers of resistance, the militant body *is* a power of resistance. Through enactments of violence — self-directed, other-directed and/or property-directed — which are anticipated, threatened or actual, the militant body is constructed as a formation of political agency. In the sense of body discussed by Eugene Halton (1995) as an ability to "body forth" meaning, the militant body bodies forth political meaning. Feelings, emotions, lived and living experiences of oppression and resistance, even bodily secretions such as adrenaline and sweat, are brought directly to bear upon a political struggle. Theirs is the 'hot' struggle of passions, far removed from the tepid bodies and deliberating 'Cartesian heads' of institutional politics. This is not to say, however, that the militant body is headless or mindless, rather, the rationality of militant actions simply more directly and patently rests upon bodily lived/living experiences — the body is impreacted in a more immediate sense to the rationality of militant action, which while rational, is not necessarily 'reasonable' action.

The overriding theme in the work of anthropologist Mary Douglas (1970 and 1973) is that the principle response to disorder is systematic classification: the creation of ordered categories which both explain disorder and restore order and where the human body has historically been the principle medium of classification. The idea that the body is the central metaphor of political and social order has assumed axiomatic status in sociology and political theory. In the corpus of Foucault's work, bodies are acted *upon* in discursively constituted institutional settings. The body is the passive recipient of oppressive power techniques. However, a developed theory of the body in connection with social and political action has been largely neglected. Agency, most often conceived in terms of rational economic theory — decision-making agents — is bodiless. At best the body became part of the conditions of action, perceived as an environmental constraint. In this chapter we will return the body to militant political agency, the bodying forth of political and social 'disorder'. We will investigate here the militant bodies of political dissent on two heuristic levels of analysis. Firstly, emphasis will be placed upon *the event,* the bodying forth of dissent — the body's direct political agency — and secondly, the emphasis will be placed upon *the meaning,* the function and meaning of the body(ies) in militant politics — the representations of political meaning symbolically/materially embodied in militant actions, communicated to the public as well as their adversaries. (See Riceour, 1981 for the event/meaning distinction) And which unlike the more rigidly codified signs within systems of language, embodied signs are more open for a manifold of 'readings' or interpretations in the context of a continuing dynamic process of interpretation.[1] Pressing the argument further, Landzelius (1998) contends that "the mute choreography of hunger striking" (what we will discuss later as an example of the vulnerable body of political dissent) "contests the representational hegemony of language".

However, the distinction between event and meaning is but heuretical. Event and meaning are extrapolates of one another. According to Allen Feldman (1991):

---

1 This understanding is influenced by the pragmatic semiotics developed by C. S. Peirce (1992) rather than the structualism of Saussure, his contemporary. Rochberg-Halton (1992) points out that it is first with the semiotics of Peirce that temporal concerns enter the theories of 'the sign'. He argues that while Saussure considered the system of signs to be exhausted by concept and symbol in a dyadic structure, Peirce emphasized the diachronic, contingent aspect of meaning. Rather than a dyadic structure, Peirce understood the system of signs as a 'triadic process' which included the situated cognition of human beings. (See also Eco, 1995). Subsequently, Peircian semiotics is a valuable point of departure for an analysis of human bodily agency.

[t]he event is not what happens, the event is that which can be narrated. The event is action organised by culturally situated meanings. (p. 14)

The event is an enacted narrative. The politicised militant body enacts and re-enacts political discourse. The body is the central medium of the political instant in the body's intervention in historicity. Power, in Foucaltian terms, becomes spatialised on the body as a genesis for historical agency — subjectification — which in turn re-enacts upon the militant group/action network, the social movement in general, and the state.

Although not dealt with in this chapter we have the militarised rational bodies of terrorists, both the 'cold' rationality of *the violent body* of a terrorist, highly trained and disciplined as a striking weapon against the perceived enemy in subversive clandestine attacks, as well as the 'warm' rationality of *the violated body* of suicide bombers which, as a proof of their commitment to the struggle, 'open' their bodies, as well as their victims, in a joint mutilated death. (See Nedelmann and Unguru, 1998) Terrorist actions communicate political messages. For the terrorist it is not their victims in themselves that are important, but rather it is their message that matters. Their victims are merely the instrumental bearers of their message, which is directed to the public and their adversaries. (Schmid and de Graaf, 1982: 13-18) One can say, "their message is written in the blood of their victim". (Heradstveit and Bjørgo, 1992: 123) The vulnerable bodies of their victims, the political artefacts of an embodied act of violence, are the 'middlemen' in the process of political communication, and in so doing, the victims author history, they too are political agents.

In addition to the other-directed violence of terrorist bodies we have the self-directed violent bodies of militant political resistance which through spatial and temporal strategies attempt to control space for a certain duration or point in time — *the vulnerable bodies* of political dissent. In contrast with the bodies of terrorists, these militant bodies play upon the vulnerability of her/his own body and not the vulnerability of the bodies of their victims. These actions do not employ the instrument of the victim's body in the process of political communication, rather, the activists' own bodies are 'put on the line' as a symbolic gesture of moral commitment to the struggle. It is the vulnerable body of the activist, which bears the message directly to the public and their adversaries. We have *the massed bodies* of political dissent. And lastly, we have *the moralised, self-disciplined bodies*, the symbolically inscribed bodies of political militants and the ways in which they imprecate the body with the symbols of their struggle, the body *as* militant political language or text. In the following pages we will elaborate upon each of these latter three militant 'bodies'.

The Vulnerable Bodies of Political Dissent

Zygmunt Bauman (1999) takes up a theme originally dealt with by Paul Ricoeur, that of the paradox arising within the universe of cultural discourse between autonomy and vulnerability. Citing Ricoeur, Bauman points out that:

> the autonomous human being cannot but be fragile; there can be no autonomy without fragility (i.e. without the absence of a solid foundation, without under-determination and contingency); autonomy is a feature of the fragile, vulnerable being. (p. xv)

Bauman argues that sociologically speaking, the pair autonomy/vulnerability reflects the polarisation of "capacity and incapacity, resourcefulness and the lack of resources, power and powerlessness of self-assertion". (Ibid.) The modern condition is one under which the continuum between these two poles and how human individuals place them within the map of this modern paradox is forever wrought with continuous negotiations and struggle. Bauman discusses this paradox in terms of how it is conceived as a problem for philosophy, which is bound to treat all ambivalence as a challenge to reason. But if we translate this paradox, the intimate relationship between autonomy and vulnerability or fragility, to the underlying continuum along which political discourse and practices are formulated we are confronted with a similar 'problem' — the political course between power and control and power and the freedom to challenge that control, between oppression and resistance, is equally a site of ongoing negotiations and struggle. The question posed here is how political autonomy is embodied in the very fragility of the body in the politics of political militancy. In other words, how the vulnerability of the body is translated as an agent of political struggle and the achievement of autonomy — how the kinship between fragility and autonomy is appropriated in the embodied political discourse of militant action.

Time is 'of essence' in political struggle. Political activists develop temporal practices, often in conjunction with spatial practices, which are designed to control the time of the event and which use the vulnerability of the body as a means to achieve political ends. Spectacular temporal innovations have been developed by militant eco-protesters in Britain and are being imitated by other militant activists in political struggles throughout Europe. British eco-protesters have successfully used new, effective and imaginative tactics as primarily a means to prolong a non-violent occupation of, for example, road development sites, quarries, city streets and the Manchester airport development. These technical innovations include 'lock-ons' (activists place their arm in a rubber tube clipping their wrist onto a metal bar and then embedding the bar in concrete), walkways (ropes strung at a height between trees or houses which allow protesters to quickly move around above ground level), tripods (scaffolding poles around 10 metre in length formed into a tripod from which activists can be suspended), and tunnels. These technical action innovations have begun to spread throughout the continent, by antinuclear protesters in Germany and by eco-protesters in Sweden. Brian Docherty (1997) tells of what could perhaps be regarded as the apogee of eco-protest technical virtuosity when in the protest actions at Newbury a tripod was erected at the top of a tree from which a barrel of concrete was suspended with a protester locked-on. (p. 8) Common to these tactical innovations by the eco-protesters was their manufacture of bodily vulnerability. These tactics do not oppose force with force, "but places the responsibility for the protester's safety in the hands of the authorities" (Ibid. 11) which has proved to be an effective tool for delaying eviction and thereby prolonging the temporal action space of a militant protest in a liberal democracy, as well as enhancing the dramatic impact of the event. Indeed, as Docherty argues:

> [b]y prolonging evictions and creating a confrontation with the authorities which can last for weeks or even months, rather than the few hours duration of most protest actions, they have captured significant amounts of public attention. One of their clearest successes has been in making and sustaining a dramatic news story. (p. 1)

When we speak of the tempo of the action event we are borrowing a term from music theory where it refers to the rate or speed at which a piece is performed. Tempo is further distinguished with a variety of nonquantitative tempo marks: *largo* or *adagio* to suggest a slow tempo, *allegro* or *presto* for fast tempos, *accelerando* or *ritardando* for changing tempos. Furthermore, there is a directive called *tempo rubato* — literally translated as "stolen time" or according to the *Webster's New Twentieth Century Unabridged Dictionary*, "borrowed time" — which calls for a give-and-take in tempo between the two hands. The tactical innovations of eco-protesters intervenes with the action event to induce a *tempo rubato* — a tempo which in a sense 'steals' the time of the police in order to prolong the duration of the event. The police in their turn would like the 'operation' to end as quickly as possible. By 'stealing' time the activists intervene in historical time and demonstrate their ability to regulate time.

When militant political actions play upon the vulnerability of the body as a tactic for political communication, the actions must fulfil two functions: firstly, it must awaken attention, capture the imagination of the public through the words and images transferred through mass media (the event); secondly, the action must mediate a political message (the meaning). The former function appears to be the easiest to achieve for imaginative militants willing to play upon the vulnerability of their bodies. By injecting the event with a *tempo rubato* the activists can draw out the pace of the event in order to allow for the arrival of the mass media. The tactical innovations which have emerged within the radical ecology movement in Britain provide us with dramatic examples of militant activists creatively controlling the temporal action space of protest, which if for nothing else is essential for their successful intervention in mass media, thereby capturing the public's attention (the first function). The latter function is far more difficult to fulfil, their success in mediating their message hinges upon the fact that it is their own bodies which 'are put on the line'. The credibility of their intentions and the moral authority of the protesters are inscribed upon the frailty of their bodies. And unlike the meta-narrative conveyed by terrorism — fear — the meta-narratives embodied in the vulnerable bodies of militant activists — commitment — requires the preposition *to*, which governs the meta-narrative of 'commitment' by providing it with a direction. Fear is more nebulous. It can imply a more general sense of dread, impending danger for (...), in short, fear does not need a direction in order to become meaningful for their adversaries and/ or the public. Communicating a general sense of apprehension among the public at large can successfully relay the terrorists intentions with their violent actions. The militant activists who risk their own lives and bodies, who commit their bodies *to* a struggle *for* a cause, must attempt a closer link between the action events and the meanings embodied in these events, making explicit for what/whom they are risking their lives for, why they are risking their lives, and to who their demands are addressed. The connection between the action event and the meaning mediated is a central concern for militant activists utilising the vulnerability of the body — their bodily commitment must be explicitly explained. According to Roger, an antifascist activist, if actions are not followed up with more theoretical explanations, then the practices of direct action can easily develop into "a sort of actionism", that is, actions have a self-contained meaning where the "perpetual solution for everything is to simply destroy everything". However, whether their risky actions are interpreted by the public as fanaticism or as an expression of commitment and the seriousness of the political issue at hand is another matter. The symbolic use of their bodies in the action (at best) conveys to the public a sense of the moral commitment of the activists in their struggle (the second function).

Another example of militant high-risk actions, which play upon the vulnerability of the body and the discourse of autonomy, are Plowshare actions of civil disobedience. When Plowhare activists enter, for example, an arms plant and symbolically 'disarm' a weapon(s), await arrest, and take the risk of serving a prison sentence in the hopes of instigating a dialogical space for (re)negotiations over the production and distribution of military arms, they are committing their bodies to possible incarceration for their struggle — the relinquishment of the autonomy of physical bodily freedom of movement; the terrain of resistance is displaced to the heart of society's coercive apparatus. Their actions induce a *tempo rubato* upon the struggle, borrowing time from society's coercive apparatus to prolong the action event (which includes the actual symbolical disarmament action, their arrest, trial, and eventual prison sentence), which is in turn tightly interwoven with the meaning(s) they communicate.

By constructing arrest, trial, and prison incarcement into their ritual action events, Plowshare activists extend the political field to society's juridical-administrative apparatus, to the very reaches of its depth in the confinement of a prison cell. Through this transformation of the political topos, by establishing a tactical equivalence between non-violent civil disobedience in the outside world and political action in a prison, they insert the Plowshare Movement into an emblematic and sacrificial structure of action. The body of an activist, once subjugated to a prison term, is invested with a sacrificial narrative. Not surprisingly, their critics claim that Plowshare activists construct a 'cult of martyrdom' which the media readily translates into a personality cult of movement leadership. These activists' status, both internally, and through media mediation, within the wider public debate, is measured by the length of the prison terms they serve. (Peterson and Thörn, 1994) In other words, bodily commitment to their struggle enhances their personal power base.

Yet another example of a temporal tactic utilising the vulnerability of the militant body is the tactic of hunger striking. (e.g. Landzelius, 1998 and Feldman, 1991) Bryan S. Turner (1996) has pointed out that eating can be conceived as a fundamental 'body technique' which both has a physiological function, as well as being heavily mediated by culture. Control over one's eating involves a degree of autonomy and refusing to eat is an act of rebellion. (p. 176) The enactment of rebellion is collapsed on and within the political field of power of an individual body. The hunger striker disengages her/his body from the collective body of the movement in order to construct its own specialised field of political action. The rebellion is a radical process of interiorisation of an enactment of auto-violence — self-consumption.

The case of British animal rights activist Barry Horne's third hunger strike brought a new radicalised focus to the protest, as well as firmed up the sense of collective belonging of the so-called animal liberation movement, both in Great Britain and through their Internet media channel, internationally. Barry Horne initiated in October 1998 in Full Sutton prison what was to become a 68 day hunger strike in protest against the governing Labour Party's inaction in building a Royal Commission or a similar independent body to investigate vivisection, hunting and the furrier industry, which according to animal liberation activists and the Animals Betrayed Coalition had been a Labour Party pre-election promise. Horne's action was a bodying forth of the animal liberation movement's message as to their "strength and commitment to fight and resist, and to suffer in that resistance" and their concrete political demand for the formation of a Royal Commission on animal experimentation. (www.animal-liberation.net/barry/)

According to McKenzie Wark (1994), hunger strikers, by the dint of the moral authority they become, coalesce the movement around them. But they also commit not only the movement but also the government to a time, which is radically an artefact of their will. They induce upon the struggle a *tempo rubato*. The threat of the final interruption, the cessation of the body itself, brings the control of the time of the event back under the apparent direction of the movement as a whole. The artificial tempus for the animal rights struggle constructed through the hunger strike, the *tempo rubato*, committed the government to a 'deadline' — here the possible death of Barry Horne — for compliance with the movement's demands. Barry Horne sought a 'temporalisation' of history by displacing residual juridical-political temporalities and their existential suspension with the directional or linear biological time of his hunger strike. (Cf. Kosseleck, 1985:230-270) His body altered by starvation was the instrument by which he was able to posit history as a cultural object susceptible to alternation. The hunger strike scenario corresponds to the "acceleration of history, a process central to the performative interventions of any social movement". (Feldman, 1991:233)

Encapsulated behind prison walls, physically separated from the animal liberation movement on the outside, Horne was nevertheless to take in command initiative and direction of the movement struggle. Barry Horne's appeal, broadcast daily through the Internet, effected an affective alliance around a new definition of purpose for the movement, an "alignment of bodies against time". (Wark, 1994: 108) In Barry Horne's own words:

> [a]ll in all everything is going well and I'm settled into my hospital cell for the duration of this protest. No matter how long it takes there will be no weakening or thoughts of surrender from me. If that's what New Labour expect then they're going to be sadly disillusioned. *That's because it's not just me, the whole movement is in on this and we can't be beaten.* I'm the one on hunger strike, but it's all of us who are fighting. (www.animal-liberation.net/barry/, my emphasis)

And animal rights activists responded to the *bodily self-determination* or in Bauman's terms, autonomy, offered by Barry Horne, radicalising their demands. Barry Horne was committed to 'going to the edge'; his was a challenge to the animal liberation movement at large 'to go to the edge'.[2] As each new report reached the movement via the net regarding the bodily condition of Horne, the struggle accelerated. Activists could follow his weight loss, decreases in his body temperature, his EKG and blood tests, and from day 57 and onwards, reports of his loss of vision, hearing, liver functions, and his emotional condition. While the movement, and the general public, monitored daily Horne's body, the tempus of the struggle was synchronised with the rapid deterioration of his body. The animal rights struggle assumed a *tempo rubato,* a tempo borrowed from the corporeal time of Barry Horne and thereby the struggle assumed a new biological framework. Activists were encouraged by the Animals Betrayed Coalition in its home page to step up their struggle. "Now it is up to every one of us to increase the campaign; to take what Barry has done and use it for the animals." (www.animal-liberation.net/barry/) The direct action eschatology and biological eschatology were intertwined. This new action wave would, subsequently, be founded on a renewed legitimacy. It would not be the same struggle that had proceeded Horne's hunger strike. This newly legitimised wave of militant direct action would be symbolically an extension of the same political technologies and ascetic disciplines of the body that were so eloquently demonstrated in Horne's hunger strike.

A group called the Animal Rights Militia issued assassination threats against ten individuals, four of them named. If Barry Horne was to die, it was promised that these threats would be carried out, a vivid indication that the animal rights protest had markedly radicalised. In the final days of his hunger strike actions escalated, vigils were held outside of Parliament, a 'symbolic fast' by thirty activists outside of Tony Blair's home, one hour for each day of Horne's hunger strike, was carried out, and demonstrations outside of no. 10 Downing Street stepped up their intensity. One of these latter actions also played upon bodily vulnerability utilising some of the temporal techniques we discussed earlier. Two activists blockaded Downing Street, swung their vehicle across the gates of the entrance, slashed their own tires, locked themselves in and then secured themselves to the steering wheel using heavy D-locks while 40 activists held a simultaneous banner demonstration. It took the police an hour to remove the activists. While

---

2 'Going to the edge' was a common phrase used by the IRA hunger strikers in 1981. "Reaching the 'edge' was reaching the cusp of history; it was the creation of a new sociotemporal continuum arising out of the dying prisoner." (Feldman, 1991: 225)

the struggle escalated in Britain, actions in support of Barry Horne were carried out throughout Europe (particularly in Sweden where 11 reported actions were carried out in Barry Horne's 'name'), in the United States and Australia, witnessing the effectivity of the Internet's monitoring of Barry Horne's body and its appeal to the international movement to enter a corporeal *tempo rubato*, that is, to adjust its protest tempo to enter in tact with Horne's body and its impending cessation — to 'go to the edge' in their struggle.

While the animal liberation movement as a whole entered a corporeal *tempo rubato*, its adversary, the Labour government, found itself, reluctantly, more or less 'locked on' to this very same *tempo rubato*. The dialogue between government officials and the Animals Betrayed Coalition assumed increased intensity as the hunger strike progressed and Horne's body deteriorated. Movement negotiators sent the following message in a bulletin to the government and the press on the 57th day of the hunger strike:

> [i]f Barry dies it will be because the Labour Government has broken its promises to those who voted them in. ... We believe Barry's condition to be at crisis point and with every hour counting there is no time for procrastination. Barry's life is on the line but even at this late stage the government can act. But act now it must. (www.animal-liberation.net/barry/)

Government officials responded that this was no less than political blackmail and that in no way would it be "giving in to blackmail". The government's response underlines that political actions begin to live their own lives almost independent from the actor and her/his intentions with their action. Just as a text becomes independent from its author and the situation under which it originated, so too a political action, in this case Horne's hunger strike, becomes distanced from its author. Subsequently, it is possible to distinguish between "the *meaning* of the action from the *event* of the action". (Ricoeur, 1981: 204) The event of the hunger strike, recorded as text in print, as well as visual reports in mass media, acquired meanings through the "active readings" of both sympathisers and opponents. According to Ricoeur, we do not merely reconstruct the intentions of the actor and the situation under which the action took place. Rather, the construction of meaning is an active inter-play between the potential meanings of the action event on the one hand, and the 'readers' own intentions and background on the other. The political message communicated to the general public, bodied forth by Barry Horne's hunger strike, could perhaps be summarised in the words of a spokesperson for the Animals Betrayed Coalition: "I think Barry's hunger strike has highlighted the strength of feeling against vivisection and the seriousness of the issue." (www.animal-liberation.net/barry/) At least this was the message intended for the public communicated through the martyred body of activist Barry Horne. So while the animal rights movement and their sympathisers 'read' the event of the hunger strike in terms of its expression of the "strength and commitment" of their righteous struggle on behalf of animals, and their justifiable demand that the Labour Government should meet what they perceived as a pre-election promise to form a Royal Commission to look into the issues of vivisection, hunting and the furrier industry, their opponents, as expressed by government officials, 'read' the event in far different terms. Having no intentions of appointing a Royal Commission, Labour spokesmen subsequently interpreted the action as an attempt to "blackmail" the government. The same event, Barry Horne's hunger strike, but very different meanings read into the action event. Nevertheless, on the 68th day of the strike, and with Horne's death impending, government officials partially yielded to movement demands and offered a compromise proposal that was accepted. An independent analysis of vivisection carried out by the Animal Procedures Committee and the Associate Parliamentary Group for Animal Welfare would iniate in January.

The temporal tactics utilising the vulnerable bodies of political dissent have in common their construction of an *artificial dialogical space*, which more or less forces their adversaries and/or the public at large to the (re)negotiation table. Labour government officials found themselves in both face-to-face negotiations, as well as mediated negotiations with British Animal Rights activists, in the temporal space constructed by the vulnerable body of Barry Horne. Plowshare actions, which also induce a *tempo rubato* upon their struggle, with their accompanying court trials and eventual prison sentences, are designed to construct an artificial dialogical space for negotiation over the production and distribution of military arms. They reconstruct the topos of the dialogical space(s) to include a prison cell, what is most often denied as a space for dialogue. So too do the temporal practices of a *tempo rubato* of, for example, militant eco-protesters, construct a dialogical space for negotiations in that their temporal innovations stretch out the time of the protest allowing for a mediated discussion of their demands and political visions to reach out to the wider public as well as to their adversaries.[3] (Cf. Peterson and Thörn, 1999) The construction of dialogical space(s) is at the heart of militant tactics which utilise the vulnerability of the activist's own body, just as the construction of dialogical space(s) is at the heart of social movement politics in general. The difference is simply the bodily risks taken by the militant political activists. What these activists who put into play the vulnerability of the body demonstrate is that activists need not be restricted to efforts to organise and mobilise in large numbers. Through 'putting their bodies on the line' by taking exemplary actions that directly and bodily confront authorities, they can act as a catalyst for political struggle and intervene in history.[4]

What must be underlined is that these temporal high-risk action practices that play upon the vulnerability of the body require a particular political environment. It would appear that a liberal democratic political context would be a prerequisite for the success of these practices. However, these practices have even been attempted in totalitarian and repressive political contexts where they have been combined with media tactics to reach out beyond their national borders to awaken globalised institutional norms of human rights such as those inscribed in the Helsinki Convention. (See Keck and Sikkink, 1998) In this way activists have hoped to awaken a global opinion, which could put pressure upon their adversaries to enter the dialogical space opened by their actions. However, this is risky business. For example, massive global media attention did not hinder the tragic massacre in Beijing June 4th 1989, and the Chinese government did not enter the dialogical space opened by the corporeal *tempo rubato* constructed by the hunger strikes on Tiananmen Square.

---

3 An example of terrorists employing a *tempo rubato* on the basis of assassination threats towards kindnapped hostages is the case of the Red Brigades 55 day kidnapping and murder of former Italian prime minister Aldo Moro in 1978.

4 see Robinson, 1981 for a discussion of the Musteian synthesis of Marxian social analysis and Gandhian non-violent civil disobedience which emerged in USA during the 1950s under the leadership of pacifist A.J. Muste.

Massed Bodies

Closely allied to the vulnerable individual bodies of political militants
we have the revolutionary contingent where the movement of massed
bodies in the street becomes a motor, a machine of attack, or in the
words of Paul Virilio (1977), a "producer of speed", which if successful
brings the street literally to a halt. It is a spatial struggle to block and
unblock movement in a territory for enough time that the existing
powers are dislodged. For example, the fall of the Berlin Wall
demonstrated the power of massed bodies, which seized freedom of
movement in physical space and paralysed a regime too used to
meeting out "disciplinary correctives" on individual bodies. (Cf. Wark,
1994) If we submit the notion of massed bodies to the organic metaphor
of Durkheimian (1995: 212-217) 'collective effervescence' (see Peterson,
1998) or Canetti's (1960) notion of the 'emotional outburst' of the crowd,
rather than to Virilio's machine metaphor, we acquire a different
understanding of the collective experience of massed bodies as the
bodying forth of the inner collective will of the mass. (Cf. Halton, 1995:
196)   The very same surging crowd massed outside of the
Brandenburger Tor, the mass of bodies touching other bodies,
'crowded' within the square, not only seized freedom of movement,
they bodied forth their inner vision of freedom of movement. The
"transformative agency" of massed bodies, which have the potential
of reworking relatively enduring structures of interaction, arises in
these (rare) events which engage Durkheimian experiences of collective
effervescence. (Emirbayer, 1996: 123; see also Peterson, 1998)

Alberto Melucci (1996) discusses the ambivalence inherent in the
experience of the crowd, that between attraction and threat. On the
one hand, individuals are attracted to the crowd in that it permits the
feeling of being part of something without necessarily taking part, that
is, paying the price of participation. Crowd participants can 'lose
themselves in the crowd' and their ephemeral interaction constructs
the meanings and orientation of the massed bodies. On the other hand,
according to Melucci, the crowd can be perceived as a threat to the
individuality of those found in its ranks. "To the perception of this
threat the individuals respond by introversion, withdrawal, or
aggression." (p. 372) Moving in response to threat rather than attraction,
the crowd instigates its own self-destruction. The equilibrium between
attraction and threat is highly volatile and can readily shift — caught

up in attraction, a sense of 'collective effervescence', massed bodies can enter a jubilant and unrestrained, even violent, exploration of the possible, constructing new meanings and orientations; if the shift is towards the perception of threat, panic and violence can express the atomised and reactive dimension of massed bodies.

While sharing many similarities, the massed body of a militant contingent can be distinguished from the massed bodies of 'peaceful' demonstrations. A ritual demonstration, for example a May Day march of a labour party, means that the bodies of individual participants are organised into the greater entity, which is the massed body. The organisation of the individual bodies into the perceived and corporeally lived/living experiences of the political community of the massed body bears, of course, common ground with the militant contingent we are discussing here. The difference can be found in the degree of organisation and the degree to which the collective action of the demonstration follows a traditional script for its performance. The "display event" (Abrahams, 1981: 303) of the ritual demonstration is planned for public occasions during which the political 'community' and its values will be put out on display through the materiality of its artefacts (flags, banners, etc.) and the corporeal materiality of its members. Ritual demonstrations are thus defined as "traditionally prescribed cultural performances that serve as models *of* and models *for* what people believe". (Esherick and Wasserström, 1990: 844) These events involving the massed body are highly organised and planned for specific occasions. Their success lies in the will to discipline which their participants submit themselves to the traditionally prescribed script for collective action. The key to the dramaturgical staging of the ritual demonstration of political community is that through the corporeal discipline of the individual bodies movements are synchronised in time and space. Subsequently, what distinguishes the militant contingent of massed bodies from the ritual demonstration is the degree of planning and organisation — the disciplined order achieved by the individual bodies, which in turn compromise the massed body. (Cf. Handelman, 1990) Obviously this is a continuum where the distinction between a 'peaceful' ritual demonstration and a militant contingent is blurred in reality. This tension is always present in the space claiming practices of massed bodies. For even in explicitly non-violent manifestations by massed bodies violence simmers under the surface with a potential for eruption. Manning (1983) argues that the cosmos of rituals even embraces chaos; within the ordered framework of a 'peaceful' demonstration are found the seeds of disorder and violence — violence directed towards others and/or property.[5]

In the struggle for power, mass rallies are one of the most effective means to communicate popular support. Such demonstrations are effective both in dramatically displaying a group's/organisation's/social movement's political strength and in communicating their nature and goals. In addition to their value in communicating directly to the public and to their adversaries, such mass rites also have direct effects on the participants, increasing their identification with the group or social movement and reinforcing their opposition to the foes that are symbolically represented in the demonstration. According to Kertzer (1988):

> mass demonstrations gain their force through the careful manipulation of symbols, combined with the emotional impact of having so many people together for a common cause. (p. 119)

Given the political value of these rites, it is not surprising that opponents often try to undercut their effect through direct confrontation and/or to 'buy in' to the event and in this way capitalise upon its given political force. The massed body of ritual mass demonstrations opens a temporal action space, a field of opportunities, for other action networks. In this sense the massed bodies of demonstrations easily become victims for the hijacking efforts of rival social movement groups, the introduction of a *tempo rubato* upon the action event by a movement adversary or rival network of activists which attempts to 'steal' or 'borrow' the event for their own purposes. Ritual mass demonstrations provide a symbolically powerful setting for rites of opposition, for the intrusion of militant bodies of protest, which in effect turn the ritual performance to an act of what Esherick and Wasserstrom (1990) call political theatre. Unlike political rituals, which in their definition always perform a hegemonic function of confirming power relations, political theatre often challenges or subverts the

---

5 An important point here is that the 'seeds of disorder' do not necessarily have to be found within the 'peaceful' demonstration, they can be even sought among its (potential) adversaries, i.e. among the police 'policing' the demonstration or among rival social movement networks.

authority. Subsequently, the militant contingent, jostling their way into a ritual mass demonstration, is (most often) a counter-hegemonic performance of political theatre — unpredictable, often creative, and potentially violent.

Since its inception in 1890, May 1st has been the most important celebratory event for the labour movement in Sweden, ritually linking the working class to the socialist movement. With few exceptions May 1st has been the most important day for labour organisations to take to the streets and demonstrate for their demands. While the placards and banners have changed in accordance with the political conjuncture of the movement, the massed bodies of demonstrators ritually marching to their brass bands and the tones of 'Internationalen', the sea of red flags and banners — the festivity of the event — has remained, even if much of the initial intensity of the emotional involvement in a 'movement' moving along the streets has waned. May 1st is *the* day for demonstrations in Sweden; it is the "display event" *par excellence* for the labour movement in Sweden. It bears an entrenched, symbolically saturated, narrative of labour struggle.

Feldman (1991) emphasises that an event is not what happens. "The event is that which can be narrated". (p. 14) The event is action organised by culturally situated meanings — historicity is narrated. Furthermore, narratives are bodily enacted as well as written. In that narrativity can be embedded in iconic arrangements of material artefacts (e.g. red banners waving, brass bands, etc.) and / or bodily actions (e.g. workers marching on the streets), one can subsequently say that the making and narrating of history are two sides of the same process. Bodily enactment, actions 'taking place', is a medium for political actors to corporeally locate their position or nonposition in a narrative configuration. During the 1990s militant activists have engaged with the narrative opportunity opened by May 1st to disrupt the narrative configuration which surrounds the ritual event of the day for the Labour Movement in particular, and for the Swedish public in general. By 'hijacking' the massed body of the May 1st event, by actuating a *tempo rubato* upon the ritual event with their own massed bodies, they have realigned the narrative configuration and injected new meanings upon the event. Anarchist activists in Sweden have instigated campaigns to 'reclaim May Day' by organising their own demonstrations, which radically differ from the ritual demonstrations proffered on the streets by the more traditional labour protagonists of the event. The anarchists' demonstrations with black flags, punk hairstyles, unruly lines of marching demonstrators, samba bands and jugglers, are in stark contrast with the even rows of relatively silent and dignified demonstrators, red flags, and march music of the Social Democrats.

Anarchist demonstrators have not always sought police permission to stage their events on May 1st. For example, on May 1st 1998 an illegal anarchist demonstration was held in Malmö where approximately 170 activists occupied a city square for a demonstration: 'against fortress Europe and the Schengen Treaty'; against the police, 'the protectors of the rich'; 'against the exploitation and oppression of women'; and, 'against forced labour, for a citizen wage for all'. After the attack by the police forces the demonstration led to a riot in the square. On the one side police batons flailed, on the other, stones were hurled. Images of masked young militants in combat with uniformed police dominated the media that day. 137 activists were arrested and 16 were charged with instigating the violent riot. Through their bodily actions violence was emplotted in the historically peaceful narrative of May 1st in Sweden.

Perhaps posing an even greater provocation has been attempts by neo-nazi and racist groups in Sweden to hijack May 1st. These contemporary attempts have a historical precedent. When the Nazis came to power, they sought not only to build their own system of regular rituals, but also to undermine competing rites. According to Kertzer (1988), this often meant trying to remould existing rites into expressions of Nazism. May 1st was one of the first casualties of this ritual struggle. Rather than ban May Day observances, "the Nazis transformed the day into a festival of National Brotherhood, celebrating the new national solidarity under the Nazi regime". (p. 166) The red flags and banners that once bore the symbolic message of socialism now bore the black swastika of 'National Socialism'.

In 1998 neo-nazis organised a May 1st demonstration in the small community of Nora in the Darlana region — the traditional 'heartland' of Sweden — which led to a violent confrontation with anti-fascist youth and the police riot squads. Darlana was the site again for a nazi attempt to hijack May 1st during 1999, this time in Ludvika, a traditional 'stronghold' for Social Democracy. Once again violence was emplotted upon the May Day celebrations in Sweden. The massed body of a militant contingent penetrated the massed body of a 'peaceful' demonstration.

Elias Canetti (1960) distinguishes between two forms of crowds:

the 'open crowd' and the 'closed crowd'. The open crowd is, according to Canetti, the 'true crowd'. It strives to grow and it continuously demands more and more people; the open crowd ceases to be a crowd when it no longer attracts more individuals to its ranks and as quickly as it was initially formed it subsequently fizzles out. The closed crowd, on the other hand, is distinguished by its boundaries; it is intentionally constructed around the socio-political axis of 'attraction', and is contingent upon spatial-temporal aspects. It occupies place by delimiting itself, that is, by entrenching itself upon place for a certain length of time. While the closed crowd has a delimited life-span in a delimited place, its life-span is of course not merely controlled by the action network instigating the 'closed crowd', its life-span is most often hotly contested by its adversaries, for example, groups of movement adversaries and/or police riot squads. For its survival, the closed crowd, its massed bodies pressed together must defend itself and its boundaries. (Cf. McPhail and Wohlstein, 1986) Activists engaged in confrontations with either police riot squads or groups of adversaries, or both, are well aware of the importance of the body in their actions. (On the strategy of confrontation see Peterson, 1997a;) In their direct confrontations with the police riot squads, racist activists complained that the police were cowardly opponents who didn't dare meet body with body. "Shields, helmets, dogs, and horses have to take the blows." (Lundström, 1995: 146) For these militant activists it is the 'pure fight' of unprotected bodies, which is the badge of courage. This aspect has a gender dimension. David, a young Swedish anti-fascist activist, explains for us what body size (implicitly implying male 'body size') means when a struggle gets tough:

> Even if there are a lot of girls who are tough and cocky, you have to have the heavy-weights in the front. But what is most important is that you have to have people around you who you can trust. People you know won't run away. You have to press yourself together and know that the people around you, no matter how tough things get, will stand their ground.

The frontline in a militant contingent of massed bodies is a particularly strategic surface. Firstly, in a certain sense the frontline represents the whole of the massed body in that most often it is this surface which is photographed or filmed by the mass media. Secondly, it is the bodies in the frontline that will either lead or resist the anticipated attack on the whole. Hence, David's emphasis upon the 'toughness' of the frontline bodies. However, what begins with a frontline surface can readily shift. Lundström (1995) tells of the misfortune of one of her respondents in a study of the ritual celebration of Charles XII, the Swedish 'warrior king', in 1991 which led to subsequent riots. The police stopped the demonstration and cut their lines, suddenly her respondent found himself, against his wishes, in the eyes of the camera and the reach of the police batons — a new frontline had suddenly appeared. The frontline surface in any militant contingent of massed bodies is precisely contingent — contingent upon the eventual 'disorder' instigated by their opponents upon the semi-ordered choreography of the massed body. Frontline surfaces, manned by individual bodies, are constructed and reconstructed in the massed body of militant protest.

Antifascist actions of confrontation (or other protest actions of confrontation) involve what we can designate as a 'semi-closed crowd'. In order to most effectively body forth its political message, that is, fascist groups should experience fear, their actions require a larger crowd than the actions of the closed group of nuclear activists. A critical mass must be reached. Their ranks must be open to sympathisers. David, continued by telling us of an action against the 'Sweden Democrats', a racist party in Sweden, which he claimed was successful in instilling fear among the adversary when 200 'kickers' joined their ranks for the confrontation. For these actions, not only the size and courage of the individual bodies holding the frontline or boundary of the massed bodies, but the size of the massed body as a whole, its 'critical mass', assures the success of the confrontation.

However, the massed body can be 'embodied', that is, invested with somatic materiality in the individual vulnerable body(ies) of militants. For example, an activist beaten and perhaps bleeding at the frontline of the massed body can assume a martyred representation for the struggle of the massed bodies as a whole, urging the massed bodies on in their struggle. In Lundström's (1995) study of neo-nazi activists her respondents readily showed her their scars from confrontations on Charles XII day. These scars bore the proof of their long and deep commitment to their struggle for a racially cleansed Sweden. Each scar bore with it a history and provided a point of departure for their personal narratives of sacrifice for their cause. Their scars construct corporeal documents, somatic narratives, which connect ideology to a struggle to realise its vision. Struggle and sacrifice, as demonstrated by the scars and injuries the militant activist incurs, are the price they must pay to realise their utopia. An individual militant activist who acquires an injury 'in combat' becomes one of the 'heroes' in the collective martyrdom of the massed body.

Even more dramatically than the bodily sacrifices of the individual frontline activist, the sacrificial martyred body of the self-incendiarated activist becomes literally a representation of the mass. However, in contrast with the vulnerable bodies of militant protest discussed in the preceding pages, these vulnerable bodies do not construct a dialogical space within which their adversaries can enter. In a sense they construct a monological space from which their corporeality cries out to the movement and which can galvanise the movement to a radical focus in a *point in time*. These cries, the autoinscription of the narrative of desperation, reach even the ears of the public through the mass media, but a dialogical space for (re)negotiations is not constructed.

Canetti (1960) has argued that the most powerful symbol of the crowd — massed bodies — is fire. According to Canetti, fire and massed bodies ('the crowd') share the same properties: its universalism, they devour everything in their path, they are contagious and insatiable, they can 'ignite' anywhere at anytime, they are manifold, they have an enemy. Because of their close points of similarity, fire and massed bodies merge with one another and can represent one another. Canetti provides us with historical and anthropological examples of human individuals' desire to be one with fire, to revive this age-old symbol of massed bodies in the living body(ies) of the individuals(s). The recent self-incendiary acts of Kurdish activists are examples of this representation of the political voices of massed bodies. The crowds of Kurd activists which immediately assembled during 1999 to protest against the capture of PKK leader Abdullah Öcalan became represented by the individual acts of self-incendiarism by 63 activists throughout Europe. Like a long, narrow flame — the 'tongue' of a fire — these acts became the narrow flame, the 'tongue' of the massed bodies — both symbolising the desperation of the situation experienced by Kurds in Europe and the very power of giving this desperation 'speech' by submitting their bodies to the destructive flames. The act was the embodied narrative of desperation, their sense of powerlessness, in other words, their lack of autonomy, was embodied in the vulnerability of their bodies in a symbolic sacrifice by fire *for* the massed bodies.

Here, both the subject and the object of violent enactment are fused into a single body. The self-incendiarated Kurd activist thereby effects a resymbolisation of the Kurd Emancipation Movement. By denying the imputed stigma of the criminal charges placed upon their leader Abdullah Öcalan through a purification rite of fire, an ordeal which is saturated with the religious iconography of self-sacrifice and martyrdom, they seek an empowerment of their ethnic community and a (re)legitimisation of the other-directed campaign of violence it will ultimately ignite.

Baker Ahmed, a Kurd poet living in Sweden, posed the question: what is it that these people say with their actions? According to Ahmed, "it is necessary to shed light upon the Kurdish language and its absence which forces people to seek after another form of expression to establish their existence". (*Göteborgs Posten*, 1999.03.03) The Kurdish language was forbidden in Turkey, it was only in the beginning of the 1990s that the language was awarded partial acceptance, however, as "the language of song not education". According to Ahmed, this is the social context for the Kurdish language where the "reality of fire, 'earth of iron, the sky of copper', taught them more about fire's character than that of words". (Ibid.) After the capture of Öcalan, it was fire, which articulated the desperation felt by Kurds throughout Europe, not words:

> That is the content: if we are not allowed to speak, then you will be forced to see us on your streets. ... That is the situation for the Kurds, to create sounds in a deaf world, not with words, but with fire. (Ibid.)

And while a number of commentators have pointed out that within Islam there are elements which privilege martyrdom and place the individual's interest as subordinate to that of the group or in our terms, massed bodies, self-incendiary acts are not solely an Orientalist mode of political communication. It can be, and has been employed by other social movement activists, for example, by a young Lithuanian student in his protest against Soviet oppression there in 1981. What they appear to have in common is that the wordless 'tongue' of a fire, the self-incendiarated body of an individual activist bodies forth *for* the massed bodies its desperation in what is perceived as a mute world. The incendiarated bodies of individual activists are powerful symbols of their struggles. They are symbols, which create connotations through processes of both metaphorisation and metonymisation. Through processes of metonymisation the self-incendiarated body of an individual activist becomes the whole of the massed bodies, a *focus* for struggle. (Cf. Jakobson, 1971; Heradstveit and Bjørgo, 1992) And through processes of metaphorisation, the flame becomes the tongue(s) of the massed bodies, saturated with the meanings of desperation, the emotionally lived/living bodily experiences among the massed body. (Cf. Schofer and Rice, 1977; Eco, 1984)

The Moralised, Self-Disciplined Body

And lastly, we have the moralised, self-disciplined body, the symbolically inscribed bodies of political militants, and the ways in which they imprecate the body with the symbols of their struggle, the body *as* militant political language or text. The militant body 'surface' can be used as a surface for public symbolism, for example, by clothing the body in a 'uniform' of collective identity as militants, by 'masking' the body as a symbol of their standing outside the norms of society, or by inscribing on their flesh symbols of their militant politics with tattoos. The body surfaces of militant skinhead fascist activists are typically inscribed with political meanings designed to signal membership in its collectivity and instil fear among their adversaries. Their use of bomber jackets overlaid with racist and fascist symbols, Doctor Martin boots with white shoestrings, shaved heads, and symbolic tattoos do indeed mediate their politics to the public at large. The iconography of militant uniforms, most vividly exemplified by the mask, is an expression of 'defacement'. The de-personalization of individual activists through the use of uniforms identifies their agency with the trajectories of history as abstract generalised forces.

However, how the body's surface is employed as political text is often contested within militant politics. While Susanne in an interview talked about how she 'becomes' a militant activist, a Greenpeace activist, when she dons the familiar overall with its Greenpeace symbols, other political activists may express reluctance in clothing the body in identifiable militant uniforms. Feldman (1991) speaks of the cultural practices of "telling" as a sensory identification of an Other through the reception of the body as an ideological text. "Telling" constructs a conjuncture of visible signs which cohere into an iconography of the Other that regulates encounters with particular others. Some militant activists wish to bypass these processes of "telling" which they argue render the others, the general public, as potential adversaries rather than sympathisers. For example, some Swedish animal rights activists argue that militant 'uniforms', whether this might be black clothing, ski masks, or punk hairstyles, alienates the general population and obstructs the mediation of their political meanings. How the militant body surface is inscribed with political meaning, what it 'tells' the viewing public, is an issue of ongoing negotiations.

The surface of the body utilised as political text is perhaps what most readily comes to mind in regards to the militant body as bearing the symbols of political struggle. But perhaps more interesting for our discussion here is how militants internally imprecate the body with their political messages. Inspired by Anthony Giddens' notion of 'life politics', Håkan Thörn (1999) has developed a categorisation of action forms which extends along a dimension of individuality and collectivity. Firstly, consumer boycotts are the most individualistic of these 'life politics' action strategies, and while the second category, 'lifestyle politics', is still a consumer-orientated action strategy, it is more systematically constructed and co-ordinated among individuals, thereby carrying with it an increased potential for meaningful collective identity. The third action form in Thörn's trilogy is what he calls 'life form politics' which he argues deals with the construction of utopian alternative social institutions (e.g. alternative living arrangements, decentralised co-operative forms of economics, and solidarity movements' global trade relations) and is the most collective-orientated action strategy. (Cf. Flacks, 1988:138) It can be argued that each of these action strategies discussed by Thörn has a corporeal dimension. For example, consumer action strategies are highly concerned with what is ingested in the body and/or with what the body is clothed. Thörn's third action strategy, 'life form politics', are the collective experiences of the lived/living politics of protest. If we contrast militant political protest with the more common forms of political practices on the part of social movement activists in general, according to Flacks (1988), social movement activists more generally *stop* their everyday routines and *step outside* of their daily lives in their practices of political protest. The militant social movement activists we are focussing upon in this chapter intimately integrate their political practices of protest *within the framework of their everyday roles and relationships* — "protest is my whole life", as Laura, a 16 year-old ALF activist, expressed her political engagement and commitment for animals. In a sense, this third action strategy incorporates the consumer politics of 'lifestyle politics' and takes its everyday organisation one step further, representing the most integrated cognitive and corporeal form of the life politics of protest. Militant political protest achieves this third action form of 'life politics' in that it systematically incorporates its political meanings in the daily lived/living experiences of militant protest and engraves the meanings of political protest on and within the body itself — the militant body understood semiotically as the carrier or bearer of political meaning and political symbolism.

The moralised, self-disciplined body is in a sense a 'sub-political' body. (Cf. Meluccci, 1989) Unlike the vulnerable bodies or the massed bodies of militant protest, which lodge claims to entrance into the polity, the moralised, self-disciplined militant bodies articulate their political beliefs within everyday life and hence are semi-private performances of their political identity(ies). The overtly political performances of militant bodies are, nevertheless, inseparable from the processes of articulation of the militant body in sites of collective identity construction submerged within everyday life. Militant political protest acquires its force, its creativity, its subversiveness, and its credibility, through its sub-political articulation in everyday life — a corporeal interiorisation of 'life form' politics. The militant 'practices what he/she preaches'.

The moralised, self-disciplined body(ies) of activists internalise their political texts by weaving their messages literally within the tissues of the body, imbruing their politics within their very entrails and bowels. The moralised, self-disciplined bodies of animal rights activists in Sweden are examples of a corporeal interiorisation of 'life form' politics.[6] Thousands of pages each month on their Internet chat sites

---

6 Whether this corporeal interiorisation of 'life form' politics is a retreat from the public arena, which is the arena or agora of politics, behind the surfaces of individual bodies entrenched within the sub-political arena of everyday life, or is an element in their collective political action which ultimately must open to the political space of public deliberation, is an empirical question which must be posed to every action network which relies upon 'personal' corporeal statements of moralised political behaviour. 'Life form' politics may indeed remain sub-political, that is, remain as collective identities which do not lodge claims to be heard in the polity. However, overt militant political protest must rest (to a certain degree) upon their 'sub-political' articulation. The militant must 'practice what he/she preaches'.

in Sweden are dedicated to ongoing discussions, advice, recipes, etc. for vegetarian and vegan food and food products, drugs and cosmetics not tested on animals, as well as non-animal items of clothing. In short, an alternative corporeality is offered where political meanings, their political ethics, are interiorised within and on the moralised, self-disciplined bodies of militant activists in a form of a 'bio-semiotics of protest'. (Peterson, 1997a and Peterson and Thörn, 1999) Rather than indulging in the orgy — the Rabelaisian carnival — which is most often regarded as a sign of rebellion, militant animal rights activists practice a bio-semiotic guerrilla warfare of asceticism as a form of protest towards late modernity's consumer society and its discourse of consumerism. The young militant animal rights activists we meet on the Internet chat sites are collectively negotiating and renegotiating their bodily self-determination — their political autonomy — in their ongoing discussions of politically 'correct' ingestion, binding themselves together as a collective actor through a bio-semiotics of ingestion. These young activists are bodying forth political meaning in their disciplined bodily self-control over ingestion that is at odds with society at large. If in Turner's (1996) terms a regimen is a government of the body and the most elementary form of a regimen, an aspect of domestic government, are the forms of eating imposed by parents on their children, their bio-semiotic protest extends from an opposition to the bonding created between family members by the common table to society at large and the bonding created by consumer capitalism in late modernity.

To exemplify the bio-semiotics of 'ingestion' among the moralised, self-disciplined body(ies) of militant activists we will discuss two heated ongoing debates in the Internet chat pages of animal rights activists in Sweden. The first example deals with the question of insulin ingested by activists suffering from diabetes. This is not an uncontroversial issue as some forms of insulin are produced through the manipulation of pigs so that increased levels of insulin are found in their milk. And while the most common form of insulin in use today is so-called human insulin, which is synthetically produced, some patients still require the older form of 'pig' insulin to maintain their level of blood sugar. Paul, a young activist under treatment with this latter form of insulin, expressed the moral dilemma he found himself confronted with in the following words: "[a]m I a murderer when I save my own life by taking insulin from manipulated pigs? Is my life worth the death of pigs?" (vegan-djuretik@onelist.com). In the moral code of the most radical animal rights activists this is indeed a moral dilemma as this code equates the lives of animals and humans as being of equal worth. Paul's appeal started a barrage of debate on these pages which are devoted to 'animal ethics'. While most of the activists responding to Paul's questions harboured sympathy for his plight, Martha, for example, advised Paul to continue with his medication as he "needs it in order to live and continue the wider struggle", all of those responding encouraged Paul to find alternative forms of insulin and to adjust his lifestyle so as to reduce the amount of insulin he required. The debate reflected the degree to which corporeality is morally inscribed among animal rights activists. At issue is the life of an activist exchanged for the life/lives of an animal(s). A less dramatic example is that of the issue of vitamin supplements taken by vegan activists. Tim and Eddie, both vegan activists who supplement their diet with vitamins, challenged their fellow activists as to the morality of their actions. According to Tim, "I can't think of a single argument against taking vitamins", and Eddie claimed that he "couldn't see anything ethically untenable about taking vitamins". (veg-sweden@waste.org) These questions also unleashed a heated debate on their chat pages. Respondents from the 'Association of Fair Bananas' agreed that as far as the production of vitamins was concerned, they are not "immoral". However, they regarded the consumption of vitamins as a direct support for the pharmaceutical industry, which in turn was an indirect support for vivisection, and subsequently vitamins were deemed as immoral. Furthermore, according to these activists, in the production process the contents of vitamins are transformed from organic substances to inorganic substances and consequently become *per definition* poisonous drugs, comparable with narcotics, chemicals, alcohol, tobacco, etc., all of which are "immoral". Morgon extended the argument as to the immorality of vitamins further and pointed out that the consumption of vitamin supplements by vegan activists had a public political message that was detrimental to the movement as a whole:

> I refuse to take vitamins, partly because I don't need them, and partly because it would show that a vegan diet was unsuitable ... if one were to require pills in order to fill out one's nutritional requirements it would of course show that one's diet was inadequate for human consumption. We would be giving our adversaries an argument for the consumption of meat! (veg-sweden@waste. org)

What is ingested in the body has both private and public moral dimensions for activists in the animal rights movement. What for most of us are taken-for-granted, the use of insulin by diabetic patients or the consumption of vitamins acquires a moral pregnancy, which is at the heart of their 'life politics'. They are not only 'living' their politics; they are in a sense aligning their bodies internally with their political stance. Their everyday dietary practices become political practices. What passes through their mouths and bowels, what is absorbed by their bodily tissues, has a profound political significance for their political discourse. The template of their politically encoded bodies is enhanced by the truth claims of the ascetic formation of the body. What is often in debate on their various Internet chat pages is the degree to which their bodies should be aligned with their political position. Charges of hypocrisy and fanatism abound. Just where does one draw the line in political practices of, for example, militant veganism? How rigid should the 'rules' be? Is there room for flexibility in regards to the ingestion of some products? In order to exemplify the depth of the dilemmas which our young activists are daily confronted with we can examine the question of a non-dairy margarine produced in Sweden, a long-time favourite among vegan activists, which awakened a heated debate in the animal rights movement's Internet sites. Closer investigation revealed that the product contained 0.000075% vitamin D supplement extracted from sheep's wool. The firm responded to these charges by explaining that Swedish law requires vitamin A and D additives, and that at this time there is no synthetic production process for the D vitamin. Nathan responded in the debate by pointing out that a margarine produced in Germany did not contain the additive, but was sceptical to importing this product from Germany in favour of the Swedish product which contains this infinitesimal quantity of D vitamin. Nathan continued with the following words:

> Just what is the state of the animal rights movement? Just how fanatical do we want to be and just what do animals and the animal rights movement win with this type of fanatism? (vegan-djuretik@onelist.com)

Charles agreed that perhaps the animal rights movement has nothing to win with this type of fanatism, however, he argued that many individual activists find it easier to be consequent in their politics with clear-cut, uncompromisable guidelines. Absolute purity from animal substances is such a rule of thumb, which, according to Charles, makes his and other vegan activists' lives easier:

> If I were to continually ponder over the percentage of this or that with questions like: does it have any consequence for the 'big picture', then I would probably find myself stretching the rules more and more; in the end I would find myself eating everything except red meat. (vegan-djuretik@onelist.com)

This debate reveals the difficulty activists have in 'living their politics', as well as the problems they have in setting their principles for their bodily ingestion. These activists are out of tune with Swedish society in general and aligning their bodies with their politics, their bodily ingestion, is no easy matter for the ascetic militant in contemporary society's consumer abundance.

While issues related to bodily ingestion are central to the moral discourse and practices of vegan activists, so too are issues regarding what the body is protected with superficially. Their moral politics reach out as well as to bodily clothing. Silk is immoral as the silk cocoon is used while the larvae are still alive. Down is immoral as the feathers are plucked from fowl (often, it is argued, while the bird is still alive). Leather products are ban-leased among activists, and carrying the moral argument even further, so too clothing and foodstuffs containing the red dyes, cochineal and carmine, which are extracted from the Mexican insect dactylopius coccus and are subsequently deemed immoral.

These debates, which ultimately resonate with existential questions as to the sanctity of life, have direct bodily implications for the everyday political practices of vegan and animal rights activists. After a perusal of their Internet chat pages it would appear as if they are carried on *ad infinium*.[7] However, there is an important political dimension to these

---

7 The moral issues of sanctity of life negotiated and renegotiated by the animal rights movement extends beyond issues of bodily consumption and ingestion to such explosive issues as the right to free abortion, a cornerstone issue for the Swedish feminist movement. These debates appear and reappear on their Internet sites, the particular debate I will examine more closely here took place during November 1998 on the vegan animal ethics mailing list and involved 15 different discussants, and surprisingly enough, 14 were men. Lasse iniated the debate by categorically maintaining that he was against abortion on the grounds of the immorality of taking lives. His statement unleashed the debate, however, few were willing to side with

negotiations and re-negotiations as to practices of bodily consumption. Through their bodily practices of integrating their moral position corporeally they are 'bodying forth' new political meanings and are challenging their social environment to reconsider notions of life and its sanctity which are most often taken-for-granted. They are communicating their political messages through the exemplary actions of their bodily practices.

According to Turner (1996):

> [a]lthough the body is an environmental limit over which human beings do not have total control, it is also the case that, through embodiment, they exercise some form of corporal government. They practice in, on and through their bodies. (p. 230)

Animal rights activists, practising a bio-semiotics of protest in, on and through their bodies, are challenging the dominant codes of consumer societies through the moral exemplary of disciplined bodily self-determination — carefully monitoring what they ingest internally — practices *in* the body — and with what they protect the body externally — practices *on* the body. And in societies where, according to Turner, the regimen of the bodies is no longer based on a principle of ascetic restraint, "but on hedonistic calculation and the amplification of desire" which promotes the body in the "interests of commercial sensualism" (p. 234), then militant animal rights activists are engaging the regimen of the body *through* their rebellious bodily practices of ascetic restraint.

A further example of the moralised, self-disciplined militant body can be observed among the practitioners of the principles of Gandhian

---

his position in opposition to the feminist movement. The overwhelming majority underlined women's right to decide over their own bodies as being what they considered a cardinal principle that must be integrated in the animal rights movement as it is in the feminist movement. Nevertheless, some respondents, while supporting in principle the right to free abortion, did point out the fundamental conflict of interest inherent in the issue. Jonathan wrote:

[n]ow don't missunderstand me, I am absolutely not in opposition to free abortion. The only thing I want to point out is that we have a certain conflict of interests here, that is, the interests of the foster contra the right of women to their own bodies. One can't deny that, if we do I think that we end up with a form of hypocracy which I think is alltogether too common in the animal rights movement. (vegan-djuretik@onelist.com)

non-violence. In Sweden it is among activists in the so-called Plowshare Movement, a militant activist network of pacifists, who have most consistently employed and developed the political principles of non-violent civil disobedience. Whereas ordinary people are reflexively given to violence, or are likely to submit to the domination of violence-orientated authorities, Plowshare activists strive to discipline their bodily reactions, resocialise their action orientations, and train themselves to refuse violence and resist immoral authority. But as these activists stress, this is no easy task. The body must be trained and re-trained, disciplined, so as the innate reflexes to defend oneself and 'fight back' are reoriented to reflexes of passive resistance to authority. These activists are elitist in the sense that they claim a special moral sensitivity and capacity for morally coherent action that average people lack. Much like the moral, self-disciplined bodies of the militant animal rights activists discussed above, Plowshare activists tend to deliberately set themselves apart from the common run of everyday routine and try to embody in their daily lives patterns of action and thought that fully mesh with their moral values of non-violence. Whether these moral, self-disciplined bodies of militant animal rights activists or of Plowshare activists are expressing a retreat from politics, setting themselves apart and above the political space of deliberation populated by their adversaries and sympathisers in their respective political struggles, is an open question.

Conclusions

In this chapter we have looked at three 'militant' bodies — the vulnerable bodies of political dissent, the massed bodies of political protest, and the moralised, self-disciplined bodies of militant activists — and the ways in which the body 'embodies' social movement struggle, whereby political space attains a concentrated, accelerated corporeal formation and a heightened level of semantic expansion; how the body is implicated in radical political resistance and political narratives are 'bodied forth'. The space of political enactment shrinks upon the militant body — its most extreme cases being the self-directed violence of the hunger striker and the self-incendiarated sacrificial body. This shrinkage of the space of enactment or narrativity corresponds to the expansion of the acting subject — the increasing correlation of personhood to historical transformation. (Cf. Feldman, 1991)

The vulnerable militant bodies are enactments of a self-directed violence, therein rests the truth claims of their political narratives. Putting their bodies on the line in a struggle, or even 'going to the edge', the activists intervene in historical time, inducing a *tempo rubato* upon the political conflict. Through self-directed violence the body and its materiality is semioticized in order for it to feed back narratives of historical transformation and political dominance that (at best) duplicate ideological discourse. However, while their self-directed violence enables and enacts an isomorphism between discourse and their bodies — "an instrumental imaginary" (Feldman, 1991) — this isomorphism is unstable, threatened and made contingent by the excess effects of the very self-directed violence that institutes the one-to-one correspondence between ideology and their bodies. Their self-directed violence can, for example, lead to property-directed violence and even other-directed violent enactments. As we saw in the case of Barry Horne's hunger strike, while it was self-directed violence and bore connotations of pacifist and religious iconography, his self-directed violent enactment led to death threats against six targeted individuals. Massed bodies, whether they are bodying forth a Gandhian enactment of non-violent civil disobedient narrativity or not, acquire their political force through the potential for other-directed and/or property-directed violence they present. Massed bodies, intervening in time on space, can erupt in other-directed and/or property-directed violent enactments. The massed body is inscribed with violence — anticipated, threatened or actual. Massed bodies can, and often are, a prelude to violence directed to others and to property.

According to *Webster's New Twentieth Unabridged Dictionary*, a militant is an individual "engaged in war", with a "combative or warlike disposition", someone "ready and willing to fight". The activist bodies we have investigated here are militant bodies. The activists perceive themselves as engaged in a war, for which they are ready and willing to fight. Much like the "church militant", these activists are in a bodily and embodied conflict with what they perceive as "the powers of evil". (Ibid.) To reiterate an earlier discussion, the more traditional social movement factions and networks depend upon their effectiveness on the mobilisation of action that require participants to *stop* everyday routines and *step outside* of their daily lives. And while the militant groups and action networks of militant activists we have examined also make use of similar forms of mobilisation, they exercise their power more fundamentally by fostering historical action corporeally *within the framework of everyday roles and relationships*. (See Flack's, 1988, distinction between resistance movements and liberation movements, pp. 80-83;) In this sense, political militancy denotes an almost total integration in what Thörn has called "life form politics". Moreover, in 'life form politics', the political practices and political narratives of these practices are most corporeally integrated. The moralised, self-disciplined body of political militants is transformed into a political artefact by the enactments of narratives of asceticism upon and within it.

There is an elitist dimension of vanguardism in the militant corporeal politics we have examined here. In particular, the vulnerable bodies of militant protest tend to construct a personalised martyrdom 'embodied' in the bodies of individual activists who through their exemplary actions put their lives and bodies on the line for the collective struggle. And moralised, self-disciplined militant bodies tend to lay claim to a superior moral purity, presenting themselves as the embodiment of revolutionary consistency, adhering to 'principles' of uncompromising struggle against an evil system, never participating in the 'betrayals' characteristic among the leaders and participants in other social movement factions and action networks. And while these possible anti-democratic tendencies are existent in the militant corporeal politics of dissent, to one-sidedly condemn them does not satisfy the need to find morally coherent and practically effective ways for radical dissent, bodily commitment, and embodied principle to be expressed. According to Flacks (1988):

> the capacity of individuals and relatively small groups to push beyond the boundaries of popular consciousness, to extend the limits of action spaces and the perimeters of political discourse, to exemplify standards of conduct that are morally superior to those taken-for-granted in everyday life, must be nurtured if social and cultural change is to take place. (p. 173)

4 The Militant Politics of Secrecy

Stellan Vinthagen, a leading figure within the Swedish Plowshare Movement, initiated a heated debate within the pages of *Syndicalisten* and *Brand*, the newspapers of the Swedish Syndicalism movement, respective, the radical left. Vinthagen wrote a polemical article on Animal Liberation Front and political militancy in general. He argued that undemocratic forces must not appropriate the struggle for human and animal rights. Therefore, we must become aware of the need for a non-violent and open struggle. While these militant movements using violent means and secret organisational forms developed in England and on the European continent, according to Vinthagen, their methods and ideology have spread to the Swedish radical left. Vinthagen argues provocatively that AFA (Anti-Fascist Action) and SUF (the Syndicalism Youth Association) have become more or less "terrorist" organisations. "These underground movements [AFA and SUF] are at worst simply terrorist youth schools". (*Syndikalisten*, no. 1-2, 1996) He continues by saying that when the Swedish left is dominated by groups like SAC (Syndicalism Association) and the Left Party, which despite their demands for radical social change remain within the 'law', then it is not surprising that groups appear which use anti-democratic methods in their struggle for a new society. "Then we get underground movements which haunt society's sewers, where they can neither create nor live, just survive." (Ibid.) Not surprisingly, Vinthagen's article awoke a stream of criticisms. However, his article did focus upon two recurrent conflictual themes within the radical left which have long divided the left movement as a whole in Sweden: the use of violence in the struggle and the principle of openness. The use of violent, respective non-violent, measures in their struggle have been a central conflictual theme throughout the history of the radical left in Sweden. And it is still actual today within the alternative political culture in general.

Neglected in my earlier analyses was the role secrecy plays for the collective identity construction of neo-sects. In this chapter I will focus upon the second conflictual theme, that of the principle of openness in the struggle, more specifically, *the place of secrecy in radical political struggle.* The analysis will build upon the work of Georg Simmel, who more than any other social theorist has conceptualised the secret society as a specific form of sociality. *All* political groups, which engage in a struggle against dominant institutions and norms in a society, must walk a tightrope between the principles of exclusiveness and inclusiveness, between secrecy and publicity. And these principles are intertwined.

A consequence of the shift from low-risk to high-risk activism that isolates the group, i.e. the principle of exclusiveness, is connected to the very nature of militant high-risk activism that involves *per definition* illegal actions. The illegality of the actions demands a certain degree of secrecy which is adhered to, less, in the case of, for example, the Plowshare Movement in Sweden, and more, in the case of, for example, Anti-Fascist Action (AFA).

Secrecy is a fundamental mechanism for the form of sociality found within militant political action networks. In order to investigate the perimeters of this conflict regarding openness or secrecy within the action space of high-risk militant groups I will contrast three such groups/action networks in Sweden: the Plowshare Movement, AFA (Anti-Fascist Action), and ALF (Animal Liberation Front). The Plowshare Movement is a militant peace movement network in which its action groups employ the principles of non-violent confrontation and civil disobedience in their struggle — 'disarming' military weapons. ALF is an international network of militant animal rights activists with a branch in Sweden. ALF has repeatedly stood behind a large number of direct actions to release animals from research laboratories, fur farms, poultry and pig farms. In addition, they have staged sabotage against furriers, butcher shops, hotdog stands, and meatpacking firms. However, ALF has denied responsibility for the repeated attacks on dairies, including a bombing in 1997, which they attribute to militant vegan groups. While they can participate in demonstrations, confronting, for example, furriers or meat-packers at a convention, their primary activity is carrying out direct actions. AFA is a network of militant, anarchist antiracist action groups, which employ violent confrontation in their struggle. Mattias Flyckt, a young anarchist activist, writes critically in the Syndicalism newspaper *Arbetaren:*

for all of you who have no knowledge of AFA I can reveal that the organisation resembles a network of closed private clubs. They can be characterised as a continuation of boyish dreams of secret detective clubs ála Kalle Blomkvist. Secrecy is almost more important than anti-fascism. When they do carry out an action in the 'open', they, of course, have ski masks on. (*Arbetaren*, 1994.21.10)

Neo-sectarianism, the neo-sect, thrives on secrecy. An analysis of the role of secrecy in contemporary militant groups must rest upon the forms it assumes. Secrecy is best understood, in Erving Goffman's (1969) terms, as a *communicative event*. When information is present as a secret, there is much more to the message than the content. Goffman (1969) speaks of secrets as information about information. He describes the various methods used to acquire, conceal, and reveal information as expression games, i.e. the procedures used to communicate secrets. So rather than attempting to define secrecy, or the group which is fundamentally bonded through the communicative acts of secrecy, so-called secret societies, I seek to explicate its essential features by examining the forms it takes which connect to Simmels' original characterisation of secrecy as a form that is invariant to content. Furthermore, in focusing upon the forms secret societies, *sic* neo-sects, assume, underlines the continuum which secrecy, as a bonding principle, plays in specific militant political groups within specific socio-political contexts. In other words, while political high-risk militancy requires to some degree secrecy, it is always a question of more or less, and subsequently, secrecy is more or less an underlying principle in their collective bonding, i.e. in their construction of collective identity.

The Mythology of the Secret Societies

Professional researchers and lay people alike have been attracted to what Shils (1956) termed the "fascination of secrecy". Secrecy permits the powers of revolutionary movements to be greatly exaggerated by government authorities as well as the general public. Roberts (1972) explores the mythology that has surrounded secret societies since the beginning of the 19th century. Secret societies have been intrinsically connected to conspiracy theories. These theories which attributed everything happening in the world around them to the work of secret societies held considerable credibility throughout the 19th century and their influence, according to Roberts, while waning, has to a degree been on the rise again in the ambience of uncertainty which prevails in the face of the coming *fin du millennium*. This is perhaps behind the world-wide success of the TV programme, *Millennium*, where a semi-secret group of violent crime fighters take on a struggle each week with a secret network of evil (both external and internal).

Conspiracy theories usually rest upon the notion of a secret organisation that is international and integrates its agents in many countries. Many different versions of this secret force have been identified. The Freemasons, the Jesuits, Zionists, the Carbonari, the Comintern, Sinn Fein, have all had the blame placed on them at different times. The most popular form of the myth is to identify the enduring secret societies as primarily the agents of political and social revolution. Their great aim, it is asserted, is to sap the stabilising certainties of society — Church, State, Morality, Property, and the Family — and set up a new order. While the myth has found its most fertile soil historically within conservative elements in society, there have even been left-wing versions.

Today, the perceived threat of an international conspiracy of fascist organisations kindles the struggle of the antiracist movement in Sweden. Just as these fascist groups and organisations awaken the myth of an insidious worldwide Jewish conspiracy. The secret society myth appears, as well, to have had an impact in Sweden upon the police and the Swedish Intelligence Agency (SÄPO) which have increased their surveillance activities in order to come to terms with the spread of militant youth groups. SÄPO opened a new division in Göteborg dealing with political militancy in 1996. Gotland's police made the newspaper headlines in the spring of 1997 when they attempted to register all of the school children who eat vegan lunches in an abortive attempt to survey the potential of militant vegan actions within their district. The school lunch personnel refused to cooperate and contacted the local newspapers. This brings us to an important inter-relationship. According to Simmel (1950), periods in which new contents of life develop against the resistance of existing power are predestined to witness the growth of secret societies. In general, Simmel argues that the secret society emerges everywhere as the counterpart of despotism and police restriction. (Cf. Davis, 1971) In the succinct words of Simmel:

the preoccupation of the central power with 'special associations' runs through all of political history ... the secret society appears dangerous for central government by virtue of its mere secrecy ... the secret society is so much considered an enemy of the central power that, even conversely, every group that is politically rejected, is called a secret society. (pp. 375-376)

According to Bellman (1984), the characterisation of secrecy and secret societies as negative, non-consensual, and illegitimate is contradicted by secret associations that play an integral and legitimate part in the politics and daily life of a community. (p. 140) Secrecy also plays an important role in every country's so-called intelligence services or secret services. (Cf. Negrine, 1996: 37ff) Furthermore, secrecy is an integral part of what we define as 'legitimate' politics. McNair (1995) reminds us of the role of secrecy in the routine workings of politics — so-called 'information management', i.e. withholding information is as important for politics as is the release of information for public scrutiny. Secret societies are far from confined to a scattering of militant political groups on the margins of political life and secrecy, as withholding information, is as important for what we regard as legitimate politics, as it is for so-called illegitimate or subversive politics.

For the purpose of indicating the heterogeneity of the 'underworld', Fong (1981) argues for a typology, which can incorporate this variety. Fong ends up with five categories as distinguished from two essential characteristics: means and goals. He adds a third distinguishing characteristic, the target of victimisation. Two of these categories are of interest for our discussion. Ritualist secret societies (e.g. secret services, i.e. intelligence organisations), which deny the means but support the goals of society, work deliberately for the political establishment, and their target of victimisation tends to be persons who operate against the establishment, e.g. traitors, spies, student radicals, etc. Rebellious secret societies (e.g. Klu Klux Klan, the Carbonari, etc.), on the other hand, work against the political establishment, denying both the means and goals of society and attempt to replace them with new. Fong's typology suggests three important directions of study. Firstly, it reveals that each of the secret societies is related in its function to certain, corresponding, social institutions or systems in the larger society. Secondly, it logically follows that a change in the related institutions will effect a change in the secret collectivities. Thirdly, it unfolds the heterogeneous character of the underworld environment. The 'legitimate' secret governmental agencies share the same underworld action space of the 'illegitimate' secret action groups, and share as well the same underlying form of sociation. They are in a very real sense bound to one another. Changes in 'rebellious secret societies' will illicit changes in 'ritualist secret societies', e.g. intelligence agencies, and *vice versa*. Stellan Vinthagen's warning that the existence of secret groups leads to an escalation on the part of the police to combat them, that is, special sections within the secret police are established in order to come to terms with the spread of militant secret action groups, bears a ring of truth. (*Syndikalisten*, no. 4, 1996) However, on the other hand, secret societies will in turn flourish under conditions of excessive surveillance and repression. These two categories of actors in the underground action space would seem to be bound by an inevitable spiral, feeding upon the activities of one another.

However, these tendencies are not pathologically bound, there are also tendencies of moderation. For example, Roger, a 30 year-old AFA activist who has been imprisoned for nine months for his political activities, nevertheless injects a tone of moderation when he assesses the political context in Sweden:

> Sure, I spent nine months in prison, but that wasn't such a bid deal. Compared to the degree of repression experienced in other countries here in Sweden we just haven't experienced such hard repressive measures, therefore I think extreme measures of secrecy are uncalled for. And as we Swedes are so unfamiliar with secrecy we all too often practice it in the wrong situations or contexts. For example, we don't always have to give false names in an open discussion with other groups. There is too much mysticism in that sort of behaviour which makes political co-operation difficult. ... The situation here in Sweden for activists is far from a question of going underground.

This discussion highlights the influence of the action environment upon political protest. A protest group or organisation must deal with the response of its adversary(ies) in order to achieve its objectives, whether these are long-term or short-term objectives. According to Melucci (1996), the ruling groups or political authorities *de facto* establish the "conditions of liveability" of the social movement environment in which a movement organisation/group operates. Subsequently, the degree of openness or closure of the political system, as well as the political system's degree of tolerance or repression of the collective action on the part of social movements, exercises significant influence on the nature of that collective action and its action organisation. (Cf. Tarrow 1989, 1993; on policing the protest see della Porta, 1995) According to Melucci (1996):

> an open political system may favour a pluralism and competition of organisational forms, whereas a repressive one may foster the formation of centralised and sectarian organisations. (p. 317)

In short, collective action on the part of a neo-sect must deal with far more powerful counteraction from the political system — whether this system is totalitarian or liberal democratic — which strives to obstruct, contain, and repress their protests. (Oberschall, 1978; Zald and Useem, 1987; McCarthy and Wolfson, 1992; Piven and Cloward, 1992; Jenkins and Klandermans, 1995)

The Principles of Inclusiveness and Exclusiveness

In regard to membership within groups we have, on the one hand, the principle of including everybody who is not explicitly excluded; and on the other hand, the principle of excluding everybody who is not explicitly included. The second type includes all political groups. The essence of politics is collective action (whether this is participating in a violent direct action or simply casting one's vote for a specific political party), which is dependent upon a sense of 'we' (which is of course relative upon a cognitive delineation with a perceived 'them'). This collective identity, or 'we', may be more or less strongly articulated, but it must be articulated to some degree. According to Simmel (1950), the group principle of exclusiveness is represented in its greatest purity by the secret society. However, this is a principle that works along a continuum. Even secret societies will be more or less exclusive. Their political project demands recruitment of new potential members. They must open themselves (and their secrets), to some degree, to a wider public.

AFA primarily relies upon personal contacts for recruitment, and their action network consists of informal 'friendship groups'; any 'friendship group' is free to incorporate themselves within the Anti-Fascist Action network. ALF also relies upon personal contacts, and increasingly through contacts acquired through the Internet. However, even if initial contact has been made through the Internet, personal contact is required before a temporary action group is constructed, with members recruited from either one geographical area or from across a wider region of Sweden. According to David, a 21 year-old animal rights activist, there is a "security factor" in relying upon personal contacts. These groups can vary in size between two and five members, and their lifespan can vary from the execution of a single action or several. The Plowshare Movement has a more active, as well as restrictive, recruitment strategy with courses in civil disobedience and non-violence and peace camps. After iniation in the rituals, or methods, of their network, persons are free to build their own Plowshare groups, under the condition that they follow the Plowshare rituals.

According to Simmel, separation, from society and from other political organisations and groups, is achieved along a continuum, in a relative manner. Hence, the neophyte is closer to the status of non-participant, from which *testing and education* eventually lead her/him to grasp the totality or core of the association. This core thus gains protection and isolation from the outside through the buffer of partially initiated. The lower grades of the order mediate the transition to the centre of the secret, they create a gradual densification of the sphere of repulsion which surrounds the centre and which protects it more securely than could any abrupt and radical alternative between total inclusion and total exclusion. (pp. 366-368) Of the groups discussed here, the Plowshare Movement has the most elaborately developed system for the education of neophytes and the most active strategy for the recruitment of new members. The 'core' of the group, assembled in a collective in Göteborg, leads courses throughout the country in non-violence and civil disobedience on the basis of a handbook written by one of the informal leaders of the movement. They have held four summer peace camps where life in the camp is highly regulated by camp handbooks written by the core collective. During these events, the courses and the camps, neophytes are rigorously educated and trained in the rituals of the movement. For AFA and ALF, whose rituals are not so rigid, the training and education proceeds haphazardly, through concrete action and through reading the literature produced by the network, particularly its European partners in England. Recruitment is highly selective. Bellman (1984) maintains that the ability to join a secret society is based more on the ability to find a sponsor in the societies than on any other factor. This is the case for AFA and ALF, where recruitment is primarily through personal contacts and friendship networks. ALF in particular draws upon the wider network of animal right's activists and supporters in constructing their small temporary action groups. This also lowers the demands upon training and education, as new members are carefully chosen so as to assure that they share the group's goals and methods prior to initiation in the secrets of the group. ALF insures the secrecy of its direct action groups by maintaining flexibility and a small number of activists in each temporary action group. Laura, an ALF activist, reflects over the problem of the size of the action and the need for secrecy. Organising a larger manifestation against the use of laboratory animals in Stockholm the network went Online with the details of their action which resulted in intensive police surveillance:

> Of course it is dumb because then you are met by the police riot squads, like what happened in Stockholm. There were riot barriers and riot police and five police vans just waiting for us. So using Internet for calls to actions is dumb. It is best to make contacts directly, person to person, but for large actions it is difficult. You have to assemble a lot of people.

Here Laura is touching upon the problems confronted by militant action networks in regards to their internal communication and action co-ordination. For larger actions and manifestations the action networks must rely upon more 'public' communication channels, for example, the Internet, telecommunications, and the postal system, all of which Laura claims are more or less assessable to police surveillance. So, while various measures are developed to maintain secrecy in these communication channels, for example the use of codes in letters and telephone conversations, or the use of anonymous email addresses and computer sites, she feels that the most reliable mode of communication for their more high risk actions is face-to-face.

While political secret societies are to some degree inclusive, they are, above all, exclusive, and a tendency of contemporary political identity construction, which I have analysed in terms of neo-sectarianism. (Peterson, 1995 and 1997a) Political secret societies, *sic* neo-sects, construct themselves in opposition: in opposition to the wider society, and in opposition to other groups and organisations which join them in their struggle defined in broad terms, whether that is the peace movement, the animal rights movement, or the antiracist movement. Through their exclusiveness, the cognitive 'walls' they build around themselves, political secret societies strive to maintain their *autonomy*, from the dominant norms and institutions of society, and from the norms of the other groups within their action field.

Simmel connects the principle of exclusiveness with the aristocratic motive:

> The separateness of the secret society expresses a value: people separate from others because they do not wish to make common cause with them, because they wish to let them feel their superiority ... separation and group formation are connected through the aristocratising motive ... secrecy and mystification amount to heightening the wall toward the outside, and hence to strengthening the aristocratic character of the group ... the significance of the secret society as the intensification of sociological exclusiveness in general, is strikingly shown in political aristocracies ... the democratic principle, on the contrary, is associated with the principle of publicity and in the same sense with the tendency toward general and basic laws. (pp. 364-365)

Political 'secret societies', *sic* neo-sects appear to favour, to various degrees, an image of a close community of 'elects', emphasising purity rather than proselytisation, exclusivity rather than expansion. According to della Porta (1992):

> [e]litism accomplished, in fact, the important function of making isolation appear to be a positive, self-imposed quality. An organisation's lack of support becomes a sign of superiority, rather than an indication of its mistakes and defeat. Members cultivate their differences from others as proof of their being among the few 'elects. (p. 20)

The political secret society, *sic* neo-sect, tends to regard its particular methods of activism as the sole means by which to attain their goals (and even other group's goals within the movement struggle). In other words, theirs is the 'truest' and 'purist' means of struggle. Subsequently, the political sect has a tendency to regard its role within the broader social movement struggle which it is a part of as not so much an instrument within the broader struggle, but as a 'living example' for the struggle itself. For example, Plowshare activists appear as an avant-garde who 'show the way' for other peace movement supporters through the personal risks they are taking. Furthermore they regard themselves, as expressed in their written press statements after a disarmament action, as a 'beacon of light' for the peace movement in general. (Peterson and Thörn, 1994: 32) Per Herngren, writing on the Plowshare home-page, explains that the challenge their civil disobedience actions poses is directed primarily towards the "obedience" of other peace movement activists. It is "obedience" of peace movement activists, not the obedience of the general public, which Herngren claims is the principle obstacle for a successful resistance to the production and distribution of arms. According to Herngren:

> I am inclined to think that it is the peace movement that is the problem rather than the government. The peace movement doesn't need any more followers, we just need to break our obedience.

'Hickory', the media pseudonym for an AFA activist argues along the same lines. Their action perspective is a Manichean reduction of the scene of action. In their melodramatic emplotment, the Anti-fascist Action activists are the unyielding heroic protagonists locked in a moral struggle against identifiable right-wing extremist villains and the racist politics of the "ruling forces", i.e. the state, its judicial system and "trigger happy" police, and with the mass-based antiracist movement as "impotent, ineffectual and lax" by-standers. In short, the militancy of his group's perspective and actions functions as a necessary guiding force for the wider antiracist movement which can at best 'put them on the right track' in their struggle. The group assumes almost a messianic quality in their self-perception of their unique role in the antiracist struggle. (Peterson, 1997) ALF also perceives their actions within a moral framework. According to Lars, a 16 year-old ALF activist, their actions have two purposes. Firstly, to save animals that are suffering, and secondly, to show both the general public that resistance exists and to remind others that "if they start this type of activity then we will come and release all of their animals or blow the place to smithereens." ALF's message with their direct actions includes an element of threat.

The "aristocratic motive" noted by Simmel that was served by secret society membership and outsiders' ignorance often preserved a privileged position towards 'the outside world' by limiting access to knowledge that might be used to undercut their power. (Moore and Tumin, 1949) However, sometimes in secret societies secrecy itself becomes a sign of privilege or superiority, even when much of the secrecy maintained by the group protects relatively useless knowledge. (Lowry, 1972) In Plowshare groups, ALF groups and AFA groups, the secrets protected are not necessarily strategically vital bits of information; they even include knowledge of action planning and internal relationships, which are relatively useless for an outsider attempting to penetrate these groups. Nevertheless, the aura of secrecy protection, literally often a 'cowboys and indians' or 'cops and robbers' game, imbues the groups' members with a sense of superiority. That is, their playing the game of secrecy in itself mediates a sense of their own and their group's importance or significance. The use of secrecy tantalises potential joiners and exaggerates the power it wields. This is a trait characteristic of many secrecy systems, including those associated with many governmental bureaucracies.

Since there is exclusion of the non-initiates, the sociology of the secret society is confronted with the complicated problem of ascertaining how intra-group life is determined by the group's secretive behaviour toward the 'outside'. The purpose of secrecy is, above all, *protection*. Of all protective measures, the most radical is to make oneself invisible, however, for a political secret society this is not a valid alternative. Since (most) secret societies must recruit their members from the larger society, it is a myth to believe that their existence will never be known to the legal control agencies, or to the public. Simmel states that a secret society is a group whose existence is open, but its goals, rituals and structure are concealed from the public. But secret societies' goals, rituals and structure will eventually be more or less exposed for public scrutiny. So Fong (1981) offers a definition where he states that while the static aspects of the goals, rituals and the structure of any secret society may be known to the police and to the general public, it is highly probable that the dynamic aspects of the society remain unknown. Dynamic aspects refer to the activities that are related directly to the organisational goals, the particular time and place for performing the actions and rituals, and the occupants of the various hierarchical positions. Secrecy in political secret societies is thus relative which provides them with the advantage of a certain elasticity. The examples in our discussion vary as to their elasticity. The static aspects of the goals, rituals and structure (or 'anti-structure') of the militant groups discussed here are more or less well known, they are not a 'secret'.

On the contrary, political secret societies rely on a curious mixture of both secrecy and publicity and most political secret societies actively manipulate the media to gain a degree of exposure. Without this 'opening' to the outside world, which the media provides, their political messages would go unnoticed and potential supporters could not be recruited. And publicity has even worked to enhance the importance of secret societies. Secret societies will tend to have more or less developed media strategies through with they attempt to reach a wider public by managing the information released to various media channels. Even some media 'exposures' of their secrets can be more or less welcomed by the secret societies, reasoning that 'bad publicity is better than no publicity'. Some of the public's curiosity may be awakened and an avenue of recruitment opened. Also media attention can often exaggerate the size and enhance the significance of the secret organisation/group, thereby making it more attractive to potential supporters. Secret societies in general rely equally upon secrecy and (at best controlled) publicity. Both elements are essential to the success of their goals and the continued maintenance of their organisation/ group. The veil of secrecy is most closely guarded in connection with strategic information vital to their extralegal and/or violent actions, while it may be lifted in connection with matters not vital to the success of their actions.

ALF action groups are those dealt with here that are most shrouded in secrecy. Their actions are covert, where and when they will strike are highly guarded secrets known only to the immediate members of the action group. The members of the action group maintain a low profile in the more public actions of the ALF network. According to Lars:

> the individuals who carry out direct actions do not participate in demonstrations. They can't be seen or heard so much for security reasons, so they keep out of the way and stick to direct actions. Perhaps they will take part in the larger demonstrations where they can melt into the crowd, but they stay away from smaller public actions.

Their actions are carried out in the middle of the night and they are masked in order to avoid arrest. Lars maintains that while he respects the Plowshare model of civil disobedience where the activist turns himself/herself over for arrest, which he feels shows the public the depth of their commitment; and while he is prepared himself to take a prison sentence for his cause, this would interfere with his immediate goal of liberating suffering animals:

> When you carry out direct actions and try to save the lives of animals daily or are involved in these sorts of activities systematically all the time then you have to maintain anonymity because if you are caught you can risk up to a year in prison. During that year I could perhaps save the lives of a hundred thousand minks with no problem. Well maybe I am exaggerating a little. But I can work more effectively for animals outside than behind lock and key.

Anonymity is maintained in their communication across the net and per telephone through the use of code words and anonymous e-mail addresses which they use through library computers which makes it impossible for the police to trace. Otherwise, action details are communicated face to face. Laura, an ALF activist, claims that person to person communication is preferred. Furthermore, a small circle of friends best keeps the strategic details of a planned action.

AFA action groups are more guarded by secrecy, than are Plowshare groups, and somewhat less than ALF groups. Aside from their general goals, most of the dynamic aspects of their network are more or less secret. Their actions carried out against neo-fascist shops and premises are for the most part covert. David claims that on two occasions he could recall an AFA group from another city carried out major actions in his city. For "security reasons" activists from another city were recruited for the actions without any insider knowledge on the part of their own group. Security is maintained in that "however much they can beat you afterwards there is nothing you can tell them". However, in that most of their actions are direct confrontations with racist and neo-fascist groups, the time and place for their actions are predictable. Their membership is more or less secret. They appear in the media under pseudonyms, they carry out their actions masked, and if they can, they avoid arrest. On this last point AFA activists are highly critical of the Plowshare strategy. Daniel Åman, a SUF activist, questions the quality of democracy attributed to Swedish society by Vinthagen which requires activists to be so open in their actions that they should voluntarily submit themselves to the legal system, disregarding the state's monopoly of coercive means. Åman questions the preconditions for democratic dialogue within a society that is fundamentally divided by unequal power. (*Syndikalisten*, 1996, no. 3)

On the debate pages of the Plowshare Internet home-page activists clarified their definition of civil disobedience as including two fundamental elements: openness and non-violence, where openness means that the activist is willing to take the consequences of his/her actions and remains on the scene of the action awaiting arrest. Per Herngren, one of the leading figures in the Swedish Plowshare movement, motivates openness in their struggle, in the sense that openness means making themselves available for arrest in conjunction with a direct action, by arguing that firstly, arrest leads to the construction of an additional space for dialogue — with the police and later in the courts — and secondly, this strategy of openness helps break down an individual's fear of punishment thereby helping to circumvent our obedience which he argues undermines democracy. This position appears to be generally accepted among Plowshare activists and sympathisers, however, some are sceptical to the quality of dialogue available within the court system and wonder if other spaces for dialogue which are less contingent upon the structures of state power would not be strategically "more effective". Furthermore, disagreement is evident regarding refusal of activists to pay fines or damages. In regards to this question, on the one hand, Per Herngren argues for a "total openness" which includes payment of levied fines and/or damages, on the other hand, Linus Brohult, among others participating in the debate on the home-page, assume the position that it is not irresponsible if an activist avoids payment by various means. Brohult claims that with a strategy of "total openness" to authorities in power, there is no disobedience left in the action.

In regard to the Plowshare groups, while their members and leaders are known, their goals and rituals are known, and even in most cases, the targets for their actions are known, as is the approximate 'time' for their planned action, however, important details for their actions are held secret, for example exactly when they will break into an arms factory or a military airfield, exactly how they will carry out the break-in, so-called strategic secrets. Without the protection of secrecy as to these details, their actions could not be carried out. While the rituals of Plowshare activists include staying and 'taking the consequences of their actions', that is, they are duly arrested, stand trial, and in many cases are sentenced to prison terms, their action planning is nevertheless covert and is consequently shrouded in secrecy.

It is only the secrecy of details, i.e. strategic secrets, which qualifies the Plowshare Movement as a secret society within our analytical framework. Nevertheless, secrecy as a form of sociation plays an important role in their identity construction. Secrecy, or semi-secrecy, is rigorously followed during the planning stages of the action, and this initial stage in the life span of a Plowshare 'resistance community' often lasts approximately one year.

During my previous field research on the Plowshare Movement I attended a Plowshare peace camp arranged in Linköping in 1993. (Peterson and Thörn, 1994) Upon my arrival I was dragged into the middle of a football field (out of earshot from perceived long-distance police microphones) and asked if I would like to accompany an action group to a secret hiding place in order to act as their legal advisor. The group felt that they could not plan their action against a JAS plane within the confines of the camp due to police surveillance.[1] They could not 'protect' the secret details of their action together with the other assembled Plowshare activists and sympathisers, so they drew themselves away to a secret secluded house. Their move split the camp in a heated conflict. In this particular case, secrecy and the perceived threat of disclosure, induced the group to temporarily withdraw from the society at large and from other Plowshare groups and sympathisers. And while this protective measure temporarily cemented the group together in the confines of 'their hiding place', it also extended a barrier between the group and its immediate supportive action environment. By isolating themselves from their immediate supportive action environment, the group was at the same time jeopardising its very existence. No secret society, *sic* neo-sect, can exist totally severed from its action environment. No secret society can remain totally secret and at the same time 'protect' its secrecy. In other words, there is a degree of exclusivity, which cannot be exceeded — secrecy has its limits. An illustration of this 'law of exclusivity' is the case of the Baader-Meinhof group in West Germany. They were able to remain in hiding for so long only through the help of the widespread contact net Ulrike Meinhof had within the wider West German left movement in the 1970s. It was through her contacts that they could procure 'safe-houses',

---

1 The camp was unquestionably under police surveillance during the week I was there. There was a 24 hour 'open' police presence, as well as frequent video filming of the activists gathered there.

financial support, automobiles, etc. and remain hidden from the massive West German police efforts to capture them.

The Bonding Principle

When a whole group uses secrecy, more or less, as its form of existence, the general sociological significance of the secret is internal. The secret determines the reciprocal relations among those who share it in common. The internal quality of the reciprocal relations of the members of a secret society rest upon confidence and trust. Trust in one another's ability to guard the secrecy of the group upon which the group's and the individual members' protection rests. Hence, Simmel (1950) states that "secret societies offer a very impressive schooling in the moral solidarity among men". (p. 348) This brings us to the secrecy principle as the foundation of the 'politics of friendship', which according to Jacques Derrida (1997), underlies all democratic discourses. Secrecy is the bonding principle of fraternity which is in turn constructed upon the *double exclusion* which is at work in all the great ethico-politico-philosophical discourses on friendship or fraternity which underlies democracy; on the one hand, the exclusion of friendship between women; on the other hand, the friendship between a man and a woman. He maintains that this double exclusion of the feminine in this philosophical paradigm would then confer on friendship the "essential and essentially sublime figure of virile homosexuality". (p. 279) So indeed, Simmel's statement bears force. Secret societies do offer a very impressive schooling in the moral solidarity *among men*. This raises of course a set of questions regarding on what terms women enter the bonds of intense friendship which prevail in secret societies. Are women excluded from these bonds, are they incorporated on masculinist terms, or can we distinguish feminine elements of sisterhood emerging along side of prevailing forms of fraternalisation? These are questions that I can not broach on the basis of my empirical cases. Nevertheless, insufficient as my material is, it would appear that the second option is at work, women are being incorporated on masculinist terms by the very fact that secrecy as a bonding principle of friendship or communion is in force. But if we put these provocative, *albeit* unanswerable questions aside, what is the nature of the community being constructed within secret societies, *sic* neo-sects?

The secret society compensates for the separating factor inherent in every secret by the simple fact that it is a society. Sociation is directly sought, and self-reflexively constructed, in order to compensate, in part, for the isolating consequences of continuing secrecy — in order to satisfy *within* secrecy the impulse toward communion which the secret destroys in regard to the outside. According to Simmel, the intensified seclusion against the outside is associated with the intensification of cohesion internally:

> (the member) must stay on good terms with the other members as it is much more difficult to replace them here than in a legitimate association. Furthermore, every discord inside the group brings danger of betrayal, which both the self-preservation of the individual and the group are interested in avoiding ... finally, the isolation of the secret society from the surrounding social syntheses removes a number of occasions for conflict ... the secret society exercises over its members a sort of absolute dominion, which gives them little opportunity to engage in conflicts such as result from the co-ordination of the plurality of spheres that represent open groups. (p. 345)

The relative harmony, which Simmel ascribes to the internal relations within secret societies, does not correspond to the groups discussed here. On the basis of my observations, AFA groups appear to be somewhat more harmonious than Plowshare groups. This is perhaps related to the less rigid rituals observed by AFA groups, than those of Plowshare groups. However, an AFA group in Stockholm divided as a result of a gender conflict, where the girls in the group withdrew and formed their own group. (Peterson, 1997) ALF action groups appear to be so temporary and flexible that conflicts do not find the time to develop. Also, ALF action groups tend to be closely knit circles of friends. In Plowshare groups, if conflicts cannot be solved through arbitration nor incorporated in their political formulations, then the group either divides or the individual in conflict is excluded from the group. Surprisingly enough, perhaps, this appears to be the primary way Plowshare groups solve their often-intensive conflicts. While the 'core' of the Plowshare Movement has remained relatively stable over the last 15 years or so, their followers have precipitately 'come and gone'. However, these conflicts do not significantly jeopardise the life of the group in that its secrets, the details of planned actions, can easily be changed.

The fact that conflicts do break out is an indication of the intensiveness of the group's interactions. Accounts of the *Rote Armé* describe how the groups, hidden for long periods of time, were often a hotbed of internal conflicts. Living so secluded from the outside world, their members tended to simply get on each other's nerves. In short, the secret society, more or less confined to the reciprocal relations between its members who share its secrets, becomes 'a world in itself'. Simmel argues that the teleological aspect of this is that the total action and interest sphere of the secret society becomes a well-rounded unity only through inclusion, in the secret, of a whole complex of external forms:

> Under its characteristic categories, the secret must seek to create a sort of life totality ... like the military organisation and the religious community, the secret society claims the individual totally, it uses a plurality of forces and interests into a closed unit. (p. 359)

As a consequence of the shift from low-risk to high-risk activism on the part of a political secret society, the more isolated it becomes within its action environment, and the affective relations between the sect members increase in intensity. In extreme cases the group relationship becomes so intense, that is, individual identities become so embedded in the secret society, that the activists can come to believe that it is more or less impossible to live outside it. The secret society can come to define the life world perimeters of the activist. The secret society can become their 'family', their 'lives'. A tee-shirt made in England, and popular among some activists, bears the tongue and cheek statement: "I am a professional demonstrator". While tongue and cheek, it does say something about the implications of the intensity of activism within the secret society, which requires a commitment that leaves little time over for relations and activities which lay outside its frame of involvement. Magnus, our 16 year-old ALF activist, describes total commitment and the time-consuming involvement in the life of an animal rights activist in the following words:

> [w]hile people are willing to carry out actions, they are not willing to spend all of their time in the struggle. So a lot of individuals just want to take part in the action but no one is willing to work for it. It is not just a matter of going out and doing an action; it requires an enormous amount of planning. ... It is one hell of a lot of work but at least I feel like I'm doing

something. ... When I am on my deathbed and look back at my life I don't want to look back and see that I didn't do anything for the environment or for animals! I want to influence things, change the situation for animals. Even if that means sitting in prison or even dying for the cause. You have to give everything you got!

Laura, our 17 year-old ALF activist tells a similar story:

Lately I have begun to feel as if I am one with the animal rights movement, that I live for the animal rights struggle. ... It gives my life a meaning as I realise more and more the importance of going out and pleading the case for animals.

While the intensity of interactions within the group are a result of the secret society's separation from the 'outside' world, i.e. the construction of sociability within secrecy as compensation, secrecy can be equally regarded as a precondition for sociability, a 'place' in which individuals 'can let their hair down'. Richard Sennett (1976) explains:

[w]hen everyone has each other under surveillance, sociability decreases, silence being the only form of protection ... People are more sociable, the more they have some tangible barriers between them ... Human beings need to have some distance from intimate observation by others in order to feel sociable. (p. 15)

Within secrecy, young people can find a 'place' for political discussions and experimentation protected from the watchful eyes of the adult generation — a manufactured 'free space' for the construction of collective identities.

Ritual Confrontation

Rituals constitute, enact, and reproduce the very forces they represent and therefore give persons who participate in them the experience of necessary force. Through the ritual event, the members of the assembled group 'make it' and 'remake it' as a moral community. Practices that enact moral relationships produce 'feelings' of moral force. (See chapter two) The extraordinary freedom and wealth of forms for ritual derives from the characteristic fact that the organisation of the secret society is not predetermined by historical precedent, but is built up from its own basis. A secret society self-reflexively constructs its rituals as prescribed forms, which govern its political actions.

Plowshare groups have elaborately prescribed forms for their actions. Their ritual confrontations are constructed as symbolic contrasts to norms and institutions, which govern military arms production. The confrontation, while illegal, is carried out according to strict Gandhian principles. The execution of the confrontations always assumes a ceremonial form. They may hammer and pour blood over the nose cone of a nuclear missile, as was the case when one of the Swedish Plowshare leaders was arrested in the USA 1982 and served a prison term of nine months. In an action against the production of small arms in Eskilstuna in Sweden, a group, after 'disarming' three automatic rifles, laid out a ceremonial offering of seeds, home-baked bread, flowers, pictures of their children, and offered the guards who entered the scene juice as a symbolical peace offering. Another group forced the fences and planted some seeds in an airfield in Linköping, a test site for the JAS fighter plane, as a symbolical contrast to the death and destruction embodied in the aircraft. Another group at the same military airfield symbolically constructed a 'children's playground' at the fence's perimeter. These are examples of the symbolical expressions which, while they vary in every case, are reflexively designed so as to offer a stark contrast to the norms of the military establishment. And these rituals play an important role for the meaning construction of the groups, as well as for their collective identity construction. According to Jean-Paul Sartre (1976), the security of ritual ensures group continuity by enhancing awareness of the solemnity and importance of its values. Likewise symbolism, which unites the form of ritual with the content of belief, provides members with a sort of emotional furniture. Lyman (1964), in contrasting Western Freemasonry with so-called Chinese Freemasonry, describes Freemasonry as the teaching of "a peculiar system of morality, veiled in allegory and illustrated by symbol". (p. 84) While I would hardly argue that the Plowshare Movement corresponds to an innovative contemporary form of Freemasonry, Lyman's account of its teaching of a system of morality, veiled in allegory and illustrated by symbol, is an apt description of the underlying discourse of Plowshare ritual confrontations — the allegory of symbolical contrast. Their ritual confrontations are the enacted practices of symbolic representations of their peculiar system of morality and, accordingly, functions as an affirmation of the group as a group.

In contrast to the Gandhian ritual confrontations of Plowshare groups, the ritual confrontations of AFA groups are marked by their (potential) violence. Their confrontations with racist and neo-fascist groups and organisations are symbolical in the sense that they cannot physically destroy their adversaries, however, their ritual confrontations take a strong public stand against relinquishing the streets and squares to these groups, as well as a non-acceptance of their commercial enterprises which sell the paraphernalia of fascism. Their rituals do not assume the elaborate symbolic content of contrast as those of Plowshare groups, rather their ritual confrontations rest upon violence, most often in the form of throwing symbolic stones or bricks at their adversaries, or simply casting verbal insults and standing firm so as to present a potential threat of violence for the groups they are facing. And in contrast to the rituals of Plowshare groups, AFA's rituals include violent confrontation with society's coercive forces. Often their rituals are as much directed against the police riot squads which are assembled to 'keep the order', as they are directed against racist and neo-fascist groups. During these ritual direct confrontations AFA activists bear the symbolic mask of militancy, either a bandanna pulled up to their eyes, or woollen ski masks. The mask has an important role in their rituals. In a sense the mask is the totem of these groups. It identifies them as militant antiracist activists, and is a symbolically concentrated sign of their collective identity, which signals the rest of society that they stand outside of the norms that govern this wider society. David, a young AFA activist, explains that by bearing masks they invoke fear in their enemies:

> Confronted with a crowd of masked activists they become really afraid. It is really a horrible sight. In that sense the use of masks fills a function.

The mask confirms simultaneously their secrecy and their exclusivity; hence it confirms the collective identity of the group. (See chapter three) The mask is the symbol of the group.

The question of the mask has become equally controversial in the far left, as has the question of violence. During the 1998 May 1st demonstration in Malmö, a large number of AFA activists from both Sweden and Denmark took part masked which captured of course the attention of the media, as did their violent confrontation with the police riot squad. Karin, writing on "Frihetlig Debatt" (Freedom Debate), an anarchist debate forum on the Internet, argues that:

> wearing masks and black uniforms is just a way to strengthen their own
> sense of group belonging. It doesn't lead, however, to any political result
> — on the contrary.

Rolf took up the issue of anonymity and masking in the following
words:

> [c]omrades! Put it this way: if some nazi bastard is filming an action I can
> understand that it is uncomfortable. But I believe that common workers
> who are not consequent militants shrink back when they see masked
> demonstrators. As you said yourselves, it is the political message that is
> important. For my part I am constructing a home-page on the net with
> both a photo of myself and my name, published together with texts by,
> amongst others, Kropotkin and Rocker.

The exchange that followed Rolf's and other's critical interventions
on the Internet was heated. The one side criticised their cyber-
antagonists with the accusation of being "hobby terrorists", the other
side countered with accusations of being "hobby leftists". The criticism
aired on the Internet against AFA's masked presence during the May
1st March was centred on its perceived negative effect upon public
opinion. AFA activists, in their turn, defended the use of masks as
necessary for their protection and anonymity as irrelevant. Maxwell,
an AFA signature, maintains that: "it stands to reason that masked
participants in a demonstration can hand out flyers and hold
informative speeches just as well as participants who do not bear
masks". Mirly, also an anonymous AFA signature, responding to the
discussion on the Internet, claims that the identity of the individual is
immaterial in their struggle, "most actions are carried out by a group
as a group". David, a young AFA activist, explained that by bearing
masks they protect themselves from acts of reprisal. Maxwell continues
the defence of bearing masks by maintaining that the mask protects
them from both the police's and fascist's registration and during a May
1st demonstration their masks allowed them to "defend themselves
and their right to demonstrate if the cops attack or in some other way
try to disrupt their demonstration." In short, bearing masks allows
the activists to counter-attack the police.

The mask, according to Simmel, is the most primitive way in which secret societies allow their members' individual personalities to temporarily disappear, as well as their individual responsibility:

> The mask is the somewhat clumsy form in which these groups let the personalities of their members disappear, and without which the members would undoubtedly be overtaken by revenge and punishment ... the disguise of the person suspends all responsibility ... the irresponsibility is the consequence or the symbol of the intensified sociological de-individualisation. (p. 374)

For AFA activists, as well as for ALF activists, the mask corroborates their responsibility to their group's norms at the same time that it signals their irresponsibility to the norms of the larger society which masked they flagrantly stand outside. The mask does not have a solely symbolic value. It offers the activist a degree of protection from eventual criminal charges. ALF activists emphasise the protection that the mask affords. Thomas, a young antifascist activist who was later engaged in an occupation of a building in 1996, regrets that he was not masked when he and some comrades forced a police fence with a bolt-cutter. He was charged with breaking and entering and is waiting trial:

> What a miss! I can't believe I was so stupid and wasn't masked. But the thing was that we had agreed in the group that we would act publicly all the time, so that they couldn't say that we didn't take a responsibility for what we did. For some reason people feel that if you are masked you don't stand up for what you believe in and don't take responsibility for your acts. But now I regret that I could be so stupid.

Secret politics in general seem to encourage deviancy from normative rules. Secrecy provides a cloak behind which forbidden acts, legal violations, evasion of responsibility, inefficiency, and corruption are concealed. According to Taft (1980), the executive branch of modern states often use the requirements for state secrecy as a device to hide such illegality and corruption. And closed sessions by legislative bodies may hide the influence of powerful interest groups on lawmakers' legislative decisions. (p. 44)

Furthermore, every secret society contains a measure of freedom, which the structure of the society at large does not have; that is, the secret society occupies an action space in which the norms of the surrounding social environment do not extend. The essence of the secret society, as such, is autonomy. But, according to Simmel, this autonomy approaches anarchy:

> The consequences of leaving the general normative order easily are rootlessness and the absence of a stable life-feeling and of a norm-giving basis ... Just as the widespread diffusion of secret societies is usually proof of public un-freedom, of a tendency toward police regimentation, and of political oppression, in short, just as it is a reaction stemming from the need for freedom — so, conversely, the internal, ritual regimentation of secret societies reflects a measure of the counter-norm of this very schematism, in order to restore the equilibrium of human nature. (p. 361)

This brings us to our next theme in the sociology of secret societies. How secret societies consciously construct this secret 'world onto themselves' and subsequently offer their members the security of 'belonging'.

The Organisation of Secrecy

Quarterman (1993) claims that "although power may come from the barrel of a gun, as Chairman Mao said, it is often preserved by secrecy". (p. 48) Somewhat more discretely, Simmel (1950) commented upon the power of secrecy by claiming that if human sociation is *conditioned* by the capacity to speak, it is *shaped* by the capacity to be silent. (p. 349) Cohen and Arato (1992) define power as the transfer of *selectivity;* the ability to determine what can be done and said. (p. 540) Conversely, selectivity is the ability to determine what can not be done or said. The capacity to be silent, which shapes human sociation, and which is expressed in its purest form within the secret society, is a power relationship, not necessarily achieved and maintained from the barrel of a gun, but through its organisation. The code of secrecy at work in the secret society, *sic* neo-sect, is a code of power which underlies the relations between the secret society and the 'outside' world, as well as the reciprocal relations within the group. Secrecy, understood as a social process, is both a cause and a consequence of political conflict.

The organisation of secrecy shapes the form of its sociation. In other words, the procedures for communicating secrets and the structures organising these procedures are more important for the life of a secret society than are the motivations for concealing information. Members are not bonded to the secret group by the secrets they share and protect, but *how* they share and protect these secrets.

The secret society does not spontaneously emerge in an emotional rush, rather it is rationally constructed in order to maintain its existence, protect its secrets, and realise its goals. As we have seen, the secret society rationally constructs its rituals, its prescribed forms that govern its actions and embody its goals. Likewise, the secret society rationally constructs its organisational form which is also constructed so as to protect its 'secrets', hence protect its existence, or at the very least as in the case of Plowshare groups, protect its ability to carry out its actions in accordance with its rituals.

According to Simmel, the gradual initiation of the member into the secret society belongs in a very comprehensive area of sociological forms within which secret societies are marked in a particular way. This area is the principle of hierarchy, or graduated differentiation, of the elements in a secret society:

> Secret societies, above all others, carry through the division of labour ... and the graduation of their members with great finesse and thoroughness. This is related to a characteristic of them, the highly developed *consciousness* of their life ... this rationalistic nature of their organisation finds no more visible expression than their structure ... the fact that the secret society must be built up from its basis by means of a conscious, reflective will, gives free reign to the peculiar passion engendered by such arbitrarily disposing, organisational activities of planning important schema ... it does not grow but is built ... in addition to making plans, in addition to the constructive impulse, both of which themselves are expressions of the will to power, there is here the special challenge of completely controlling a large, potentially and ideally subordinated group of human beings, by developing a scheme of positions with their rank interrelations. (pp. 357-358)

Simmel takes a rather pessimistic view as to the degree of hierarchy inherent within the secret society that is probably coloured by the secret societies that existed in his historical context. He continues his discussion of hierarchy with the following words:

> [c]orresponding to the outstanding degree of cohesion within the secret society is the thoroughness of its centralisation ... the more criminal its purposes, the more unlimited, usually, is the power of the leaders and the

cruelty of its exercise ... the excess of freedom from all otherwise valid norms must be brought into equilibrium by a similarly excessive submission and renunciation of the will. Yet more essential is the necessity of centralisation, which is the life condition of the secret society ... In the secret society with an unknown leader, the general sociological cohesion of a group through the unity of its ruling authority is transferred, as it were, into an imaginary focus, and thus attains its purest, most intense form. (pp. 370-372)

Simmel's arguments hold a greater validity for militant political groups on the far right, as well as so-called terrorist groups, than they hold for the left-wing secret societies, *sic* neo-sects, discussed here. Plowshare groups, ALF action groups, and AFA groups are self-consciously anti-hierarchical and expressly anti-elitist. However, this de-centralised, anti-hierarchical organisational principle is not foreign to the history of secret societies. According to Fong, (1981), authority in Chinese brotherhood-based secret societies in the 19th and early 20th centuries was differentially distributed throughout the hierarchical structure; authority was diffuse and decentralised. (p. 124) So too for our research cases.

All of the groups discussed here are reticular and self-consciously anti-hierarchical. Paul, a 21 year-old ALF activist, argued against the Plowshare's notion of civil disobedience based on openness and dialogue which involves awaiting arrest and taking a possible prison sentence. He argued for direct actions and the maintenance of secrecy. The basis for his arguments was that Plowshare's actions constructed a sort of "personal martyrdom" which in turn constructed, both in the media and within the action network of Plowshare activists, what he regarded as a leadership — "certain individual activists stick out". Anonymous direct actions, on the other hand, are according to this activist, inherently non-hierarchical as they are less susceptible for "personality cults", whether these are constructed internally or through the media.

In contrast with AFA groups and ALF action groups, Plowshare groups have the most detailed organisational strategy to come to terms with the unequal distribution of authority. The ideology of non-violence permeates both their action rituals as well as their organisational praxis where there is an attempt to transform non-violent principles into a non-oppressive, non-hierarchical organisational strategy. While their action rituals are directed towards disarmament of the military and the legal system which protects it, their organisational strategy is directed towards 'disarmament of self'. Sexism, racism, homophobia and other forms of oppression, which are structuring principles of the existing social order, are self-consciously confronted within the group itself. (Peterson and Thörn, 1994) To this end they have developed a number of group techniques which provide a ritualised organisational structure for an incorporation of their 'non-violent principle of organisation'. Plowshare groups are so-called affinity groups, temporary 'resistance communities', which seldom consist of more than eight persons, constituted around a specific action with a life-span of approx. one to ten years, including action preparation, implementation, and the after-following trial period. Limiting the size of the resistance communities to approximately eight members is deemed necessary for the collective communication process where the ideal of consensus is strictly followed; no decision is taken if not all the members of the group agree. To reach consensus, certain techniques or 'methods' have been developed. Ideally, in the beginning of every group meeting 'the chairman function' is divided into three different functions: the facilitator, the vibe-watcher and the timekeeper. The facilitator has the responsibility to see that the subjects on the agenda are really discussed. The vibe-watcher has the important function of concentrating on 'vibrations' in the group in order to bring up underlying conflicts that could disturb the communication process. The vibe-watcher could also be chosen as a 'mediator' when conflicts were brought to light. Finally, the timekeeper keeps her/his eye on the clock and signals when the set time for the meeting is approaching. This 'effectiveness-orientation' is according to members not purely instrumental. Rather the practice is based on the idea that prolonged and tiring meetings weaken the democratic quality of the consensus-building process. Another organisational praxis was the so-called 'rounds method', where the word is passed around so that everyone gets an un-interrupted opportunity to speak her/his mind. In addition, at the beginning and end of most meetings a 'personal sharing round' is taken where each member is expected, but not obliged, to speak about her/his feelings in general, in regards to the group, etc. — an element of what we have termed the 'intimacy of resistance'. (Peterson and Thörn, 1994: 28) Together these ritualised organisational methods contribute towards the internal cohesion of the group, welding the members of the group together as a 'resistance community' whose inner cohesion offers protection as well for its secrets. And while these organisational methods are democratic innovations, they do not guarantee democratic communication processes. Despite these safeguards, conflicts are not eliminated and often lead to group divisions and exclusions. And while the groups are expressly anti-hierarchical and reticular, informal hierarchies and imbalances in the distribution of authority do develop. Partly, this is an inevitable feature of all protest networks, which exist solely on the basis of the active participation of their supporters. For various reasons some members are able to sacrifice more time to the struggle than others are. The greater the commitment, the more information the individual acquires, the greater the influence the individual can wield. (Peterson, 1992) Furthermore, the ideological emphasis on the part of some activists within the movement upon punishment, actions that carry a penalty of fines or imprisonment, further enhances the elitism of the Plowshare movement. The length of the prison sentence served by the activist determines to a degree his or her authority both internally within the movement and externally in the mass media. The length of the prison sentence becomes a gauge with which to measure the activist's commitment to the cause of peace. This source of elitism is a recognised problem within the movement and is the subject of internal discussions. (Peterson and Thörn, 1994: 32)

The close-knit 'resistance community' which is self-reflexively constructed by Plowshare activists is well suited to guard the secrets of the group. Group cohesion and the protection of its secrets go hand in hand, the former is the precondition for the latter, and the latter is an integral element in the former. Their actions, with the military as their 'target', require a time-consuming preparedness. They train themselves through the use of role games for the action and eventual difficulties encountered during the 'operation'. It is particularly during the extensive initial planning stage that the group is both welded together as a group and at the same time welded together to protect the secret details of the action they are planning. During the actual action, they have a strict definition and division of roles and functions in the group in order to carry out the 'operation' with, paradoxically, almost 'military precision'.

On Democratic Process

Jürgen Habermas' (1989) account of the development of the public sphere during the 19th century describes the secret orders and Masonic lodges in Germany, which while they avoided social exclusiveness, bringing together in an equal manner private people into a public, their exclusiveness was in relation to the political realm of absolutism as social equality was possible at first only as an equality outside the state. Hence, this 'public' was anticipated in secret, and the initial 'public sphere' met largely behind closed doors. The 'reason of Enlightenment' which governed the reciprocal relations among the members of the orders and lodges relied upon secrecy; its 'public' remained internal. The 'light of reason', which was veiled for self-protection, was revealed only in stages. However, in the end:

> the practice of secret societies fell prey to its own ideology to the extent to which the public that put reason to use, and hence the bourgeois public sphere for which it acted as the peacemaker, won out against state-governed publicity. (p. 38)

The secret societies which Habermas highlights in his analysis as the forebearers of what was to become the bourgeois public sphere, developed into open associations when the need for secrecy no longer existed, that is, when its discursive principles had infiltrated the wider society to the degree that they had become the dominant principles governing society as a whole. Within these secret societies bubbled the future and Habermas quotes Ernst Lessing's famous statement from 1778: "if indeed bourgeois society is not merely the offspring of Freemasonry". (Ibid.) If Freemasonry was the harbinger of the future order, other secret societies, which had expressly political projects, were harbingers of the revolutionary militant struggle of the future. Buonarroti[2] sought to explain the nature and principles of his secret society ('Sublimes Maitres Parfaits' and its successor, Monde) in the following words:

---

2 Filippo Buonarroti, the 'first professional revolutionist, was one of Babeuf's chief colleagues in the "Society of Equals". He was important for its conspiracy and the outstanding figure in the history of the secret societies lodging intrigues throughout the Napoleonic period, particularily in connection with the Cabonari which helped to engineer the collapse of the Napoleonic Kingdom of Italy.

[t]he secret society ... is a democratic institution in its principles and in its goal, but its forms and its organisation cannot be those of a democracy. With respect to doctrines, which one assumes are held in a pure form by the leaders, they would be better preserved and transmitted by them than by the crowd of initiated whose opinions ... will never be altogether fixed or uniform. With respect to action, it is absolutely necessary that the impulse come from above and that all the rest obey. This society is nothing else but a secret army destined to fight a powerful enemy. (cited in MacKenzie, 1996, p. 51)

That required complete separation between ordinary members and the leadership. "The aim that a secret society sets itself ... [must] be confined to a small group of men". (Ibid.) However, its doctrines could not be spread widely without enlisting many obedient followers. Buonarroti compared himself with Ignatius Loyala, founder of the Jesuits:

Amidst the collapse of free institutions, amidst the general corruption of sentiments, one can only find ... future regeneration in a secret corps guided by a pure and dictatorial authority ... If the end is just and wise, what difference does it make if the means have been used in other circumstances for a contrary end!   (Ibid: 53)

However, these elitist models of secret societies were not always successful in exploiting popular resentment and were often ineffective. Despite the enormous publicity the secret societies of the 19th century received, especially during their golden epoch during the Restoration, they never realised their goals for revolution. The 'secret societies' discussed here, the Plowshare Movement, ALF, and AFA, suffer the same fate as their historical predecessors. They remain highly publicised, although in regard to numerical strength, they are highly marginal elements within their respective social movements. And like their predecessors, their democratic aspects remain problematical. Firstly, in respect to their employment of violence (whether their enactments of violence are other-directed, self-directed and/or property-directed) in that democracy is a touchstone for a root paradigm in societies in which discourse takes the place of violence. And secondly, in regards to the openness of their spaces for this democratic discourse.

In regard to contemporary secret societies', *sic* neo-sects', inability to attract a large following of activists, Simmel's (1950) argument on group size and radicalism sheds some light. Simmel argues that large groups, in comparison with small groups, seem to show less radicalism and decisiveness. However, he modifies this statement by admitting that when political, social or religious movements activate large masses, they are ruthlessly radical, and extreme parties overwhelm moderate ones. This sort of radicalism, according to Simmel, is distinguished by its emotionality and is characteristic of large groups. But Simmel maintains that the — temporary — radicalism of a mass is an exception, for in general, small parties are more radical than large ones, whereby the ideas that form the basis of the party itself put the limits on its radicalism. According to Simmel, "radicalism here is sociological in its very nature". (p. 94) Radicalism is necessitated by the unreserved devotion of the individual to the rationale of the group (in contrast with the emotionality of the mass), by the sharp delimination of the group against other nearby groups (a sharpness of demarcation required by the need for the self-preservation of the group), and by the impossibility of taking care of widely varying tendencies and ideas within a narrow social framework. Of all of this, and in line with Simmel's sociology of *form,* the radicalism of *content* is largely independent:

> It is the unconditional solidarity of elements on which the sociological possibility of radicalism is based. This solidarity decreases in the measure in which numerical increase involves the admission of heterogeneous individual elements. (p. 95)

It would appear that the radicalism of contemporary militant groups destines their numerical size to remain small, and conversely, their relative small size allows their political goals and strategies to retain a radical construction. Similarly we can argue alone the lines of Derrida (1997) that secrecy is very much playing the numbers game. Citing Montaigne, Derrida argues that the essence of politics is that:

> one must choose between the sovereign fraternity of secrecy between two, in the friendship of exception, and, on the other hand, the brotherhood or the conjunction of political secrecy which begins with three. (p. 184)

If political secrecy begins with three, where does it end? How many can be included? Derrida continues by arguing that in Kantian terms, the existence and necessity of secrecy are correlative to scarcity. "It is owing to secrecy that it should be said: he who has many friends has none." (p. 258) Hence, the secret society, in order to maintain its bonding principle, that is, trusted to guard its secrets, is by nature small, its 'friends' few in numbers. In particular ALF maintains restricted membership in their temporary action groups; in part because the types of sabotage they carry out require only a small number of activists, and in part because of the nature of their actions which have resulted in enormous economic damages during the past few years making these groups the object of intense police surveillance. Subsequently, being few in numbers is vital for their protection.

Lasse Gustavsson, with a background in the Plowshare Movement as well as the anarchist movement, provides another reason for the inability of secret societies to elicit a wider support. He argues that anonymity and secrecy were factors behind the anarchist movement's self-suffocation during the 1970s. He wonders "how can an anarchist movement grow and root within a wider context if we cannot, even in our own newspapers, appear with our own names?" (*Brand*, no. 2, 1996) He continues by arguing that an anarchist society is not a possibility if "we choose to isolate ourselves in small sub-cultural groups". (Ibid.) This activist argues that secrecy as a form for organisation and action is doomed to a life on the margins of political life. Its relative invisibility makes it more or less inaccessible for a wider group of supporters.

And while the size of a group does not guarantee the quality of their democratic practices, Simmel argues that in practice the social autonomy of secret societies presents itself as group egoism and is *per definition* anti-democratic:

> The group pursues its own purposes with the same inconsiderateness for all purposes outside itself ... However, in the case of a small circle, which intends to preserve and develop itself within a larger one, this egoism has certain limits as long as it exists publicly. An open association, no matter how violently it fights against other associations within the same larger society, or against the general foundations of this society, must always maintain that the realisation of its own ultimate purposes is to the advantage of the whole. And the necessity of this outward assertion somewhat restricts the egoism of its actions. This necessity does not exist in the case of secret societies, which always therefore, at least potentially, can afford to be hostile to other groups or to the whole. Non-secret groups cannot admit such hostility, and

therefore, cannot unconditionally practice it. Nothing symbolises, or possibly promotes, the separation of the secret society from its social environment as decisively as the elimination of the hypocrisy, or of the actual condescension, by means of which the non-secret society is inevitably integrated with the teleology of its environment. (pp. 368-369)

Hickory', a media pseudonym for an AFA activist and the organisation's self-proclaimed ideologist, offers us an illustration of this group-egoism and hostility. In a radio debate 'Hickory' was unwavering in his support of a series of militant actions on the part of an AFA group in Stockholm against the premises of a racist organisation where even the safety of innocent tenants from surrounding flats was jeopardised. He agreed that their fear was regrettable, but nevertheless supported the actions as they were motivated by a good cause. (Swedish Radio, Studio ett, 1998.07.16: 17.00) In a sense 'Hickory's' action analysis transgresses the argument that the end justifies the means. For 'Hickory' the means is in a sense the end — means and end are collapsed. And for AFA in general, their guiding principle of the 'supremacy of praxis', where action swallows up any notion of dialogue, does not appear to make the group a forebearer of future democratic forms of sociation. Rather, they seem content with their role as self-proclaimed political 'revolutionaries'.

The Plowshare Movement is the group that deals most self-reflectively with the democratic quality of its practices and its goals. Stellan Vinthagen argues that in principal secrecy is undemocratic. Responding to his critics, Vinthagen says in a second article that when he argues his case in court in connection with his Plowshare actions he asserts his fundamental belief in openness and dialogue, even, and "perhaps most importantly, within oppressive societies, as only democratic methods can overcome dictatorial methods". (*Syndakilisten*, no. 4, 1996) However, the dialogue, which the Plowshare Movement so cherishes, is fictitious in that dialogue is the discursive form for doubt, where in its ideal form differences are aired and brought to light in a manner of mutual respect. The dialogue opened by Plowshare praxis rests upon certitude, for example, the unequivocal non-negotiability of the principle of non-violence.[3] This particular principle was the cause of internal strains within the 'dialogue' of the Plowshares

---

3 See Beck (1997) for a discussion of certitude and doubt; chapters two and six.

on two occasions that I observed. Both involved a feminist critique that argued that while non-violence was the preferable collective action strategy, physical self-defence on the part of a woman attacked by a rapist could very well be the preferable method in this situation. In short, for some women in the movement, the use of violence was negotiable. However, this negotiability of one of the fundamental principles governing the Plowhare Movement was not accepted by the men who dominated the action network, and their critique was silenced. In short, certitude is not commensurable with dialogue, if dialogue is understood as an exchange of experiences, ideas and opinions, which in its very character rests upon doubt.

Furthermore, the question of dialogue with authorities of power is not unconditionally accepted within the Plowshare action network. During the summer of 1997 representatives for the Plowshare network entered into a 'dialogue' with executives from the Bofors Concern, Sweden's largest arms manufacturer. Opposition to this dialogue was threefold. Firstly, opponents argued that this dialogue, what Per Herngren has called "a unique opportunity in world history", was not in fact a dialogue but rather negotiations under unequal premises. The talks were held under the condition that the Plowshare network abstained from direct actions during the summer. Subsequently, opponents to the talks claimed that they had relinquished their only means to apply pressure upon Bofors to stop their arms export to Indonesia. Proponents for the talks countered by maintaining that threats, for example the threat of a direct action, are incommensurable with dialogue. Opponents responded by pointing out that Bofors, by setting the conditions for the talks, had in fact made an implicit threat. Secondly, it was argued that the talks were not transparent for the public, which subsequently, according to the opponents, called into question democratic publicity of the process. Bofors had demanded that while the fact that they had entered these talks could be publicly announced, what was discussed during these meetings must be held secret. This demand was interpreted by the Plowshare representatives in the talks that while they could discuss the points addressed internally with their various groups, they would not reveal publicly the content of their talks with Bofors — the talks would be held semi-secretly. Thirdly, it was argued that the moral basis for a dialogue did not exist as the two parties in the talks — Plowshare peace activists and representatives of an arms manufacturer — were too far apart on the fundamental issues of arms control. Proponents agreed that this was the case, but they argued that in regards to a partial goal, that of a stop for the export of arms to Indonesia, a moral consensus was not necessary. Despite these criticisms levied against the negotiations these talks could be, and were interpreted by some activists as a major political break-through in that by engaging in these talks the arms manufacturer *de facto* awarded this militant peace group political legitimacy by recognising them as discursive partners. This debate reveals that the principle of dialogue is not necessarily unproblematic for a militant peace group. Firstly, the conditions for dialogue — an equal exchange of experiences, ideas, and opinions — are not readily met when the distribution of power is unbalanced. And secondly, dialogue can not be confused with negotiations, where talks are a co-operative endeavour. Those engaged in negotiations are negotiating toward something together. They must be engaged in at least one common end, and be willing to engage in some sort of exchange — a give and take on both sides. It is uncertain in this particular case whether the Plowhare activists were engaged in a common end in their talks with the arms manufacturer or whether, as their critics claimed, they were just the victims of a tactic of distraction from their planned actions against the plant.

While the relatively small size of their supporters, and the radicalism of their goals and strategies, certainly does not disqualify the democratic quality of the organisational form or methods of struggle of the Plowshare Movement, the secrecy of their action preparations, and execution, does pose problems for the democratic quality — if democratic qualities rest upon openness, accessibility of information, inclusiveness, and dialogue — of their struggle. The very exclusiveness of their groups, and during the stage of their action preparations they are highly exclusive, confined within the 'law of secrecy', denies democratic exchange. And as long as these groups are in essence action groups, where the dialogue they so hotly tender has more the character of monologue, even when they are attempting to create innovative spaces for dialogue (e.g. in the courts, in closed talks with arms manufacturers), then they will probably not be the precursors of future democratic associations. Furthermore, democracy, for Derrida, remains a promise; it remains indefinitely perfectible, hence always insufficient and future, as long as democratic discourses are essentially based upon the secret homo-fraternal and phallogenocentric schema of friendship.

The Rational Organisation of Emotions

The Simmelian approach to the secret society provides us with an understanding as to the form of sociation, which underlies what I have designated as the neo-sect, that is, the highly exclusive collective identity of militant political groups, which are welded together during the emotional intensity of direct confrontations. However, without a form of sociation this emotional intensity — which is by its very nature, fleeting, effervescent — would evaporate and could not function as a bonding principle. High-risk militant groups are *per definition* illegal in that their confrontations are more or less illegal actions, which carry with them the risk of criminal charges, subsequently; these groups are more or less secret. If nothing else, these groups must protect the secret details of their actions if they are to carry out them successfully. Secrecy is a protective mechanism with respect to the outside world. Hence, the protection of secrecy imbues the groups with a vital bonding principle. While the secret severs certain ties with the 'outside' world, it fuses the group internally. The secret society, *sic* neo-sect, self-reflexively and rationally constructs its organisational form so as to offer protection of the secrets of the group, and likewise, self-reflexively and rationally constructs its rituals which govern its actions in order to imbue the group's emotionality with a sense of purpose. *The protection of secrecy is the rational organisation of emotions.* The foundation of secrecy both confirms and reinforces the basic solidarity — the being together — upon which the secret society, *sic* neo-sect, rests.

Georg Simmel (1950) was of course commenting upon the 'central power's' preoccupation with perceived subversive groups, *per definition*, secret societies, at the turn of the twentieth century. "The secret society is so much considered an enemy of the central power that, even conversely, every group that is politically rejected, is called a secret society". (p. 376) How relevant are his observations at the turn of the 21st century? The intelligence operations of contemporary states give support to Simmel's view that secrecy tends to breed more secrecy. Taft (1980) claims that recent events have demonstrated that modern democratic governments have increased secret surveillance of their citizens, using the techniques of foreign espionage.

Of great concern to governments is the possible use of dissident political organisations by foreign agents for subversive ends. It is understandable why secret orders still provoke such suspicion. Secrecy, indeed, breeds the suspicion by outsiders that activities, which must be hidden, are likely illegal, immoral, or subversive. Moreover, the secret society being a power separate and independent of state government is often considered a threat by political leaders unless they can establish control over it or discover its true plans and have knowledge of its activities. (p. 59) Taft argues that even relatively 'open' associations are subject to much government surveillance and espionage.

Both David Lyon (1994) and Gary T. Marx (1986), among others, warn that the development of contemporary information technologies have had enormous implications for the extension and denseness of the surveillance capacity of modern states. 'Authoritarian potentials' resulting from information technologies exist *within* democratic societies — Marx's 'iron fist in the velvet glove'. Lyon (1997) maintains that:

> such authoritarian potential, though present for all citizens, is especially likely to be realised in relation to political dissidents, minorities, and the poor. (p. 88)

For example, in Germany the *Verfassungsschutz* (Department of the Protection of the Constitution) keeps files on all who in any way criticise the government. In Canada the Security Intelligence Service has been severely criticised for intruding on the lives of too many Canadians' because of its observing of left wing, peace activist and environmental groups. (Lyon, 1997: 115) Sweden is no exception. Its augmented surveillance capacities with the use of information technology, arguably the technologically most advanced surveillance society in the world, have been employed by its intelligence agency (SÄPO) to map the activities of dissident groups on a scale which has been seldom subjected to democratic accountability. Dennis Tollberg, a Swedish law professor, severely criticises SÄPO's arbitrary definition of 'national security risk', which he argues has led to the persecution of first left-wing dissidents, and now even more unmercifully, the persecution of certain ethnic minorities residing in Sweden. Despite these scandals, which the Swedish media has brought to light, Tollberg points a warning finger towards the leading political parties' reluctance to investigate democratic infringements in SÄPO's activities thereby placing the state's security service under democratic accountability.

Secrecy, in the name of a diffuse alleged 'national interest', has subsequently remained largely unchallenged. (*Göteborgs Posten*, 1997.07.05) The fact that an increasing number of dissident groups in Sweden employ secrecy (more or less) can to some degree be regarded as a result of this increased state surveillance. The political map of 'association Sweden', with its proliferation of 'open associations' dominating its political culture and corporate structure, has radically changed its contours since the late 1960s and perhaps even more radically today. Secrecy, practised by both the state and its political critics, appears to be an entrenched insidious political feature this society will have to actively confront if its democratic qualities are to be defended and enriched.

5 Political Militancy in Media Modernity

The struggle to make oneself heard or seen is not a peripheral aspect of the social and political upheavals of complex societies; on the contrary, it is central to them. The struggle to capture the attention of media audiences is essential for an understanding of contemporary political militancy. Militant groups/action networks are locked within a struggle over 'meaning' which increasingly finds its forum within the mediated publicness opened by the media, historically with the development of print media and today with the expansion of this space of visibility with the advent and development of electronic media. Militant groups today are increasingly staging their actions as media events, in the general tendency towards the aesthetisation of politics, in order to occupy this space of visibility which is both opening and expanding in our period of what we designate as media modernity. (Peterson and Thörn, 1994) The media spreads the influence of militant actions and disseminates their messages within a mediated publicness where to paraphrase Todd Gitlin (1980), 'the whole world is watching' — simultaneously. Militant groups/action networks stage events in order to gain access to the public imagination through the mass media. In a sense, media events are irruptions in the routine occurrence of news. As Manning (1996) has pointed out, media events have become central to contemporary political experience. In his terms, media events are dramatically staged events which use the media's stylised forms and are informed by media logic. They are political events that employ media's power to amplify in political significance activities that might otherwise be invisible and their messages obscure. (Cf. Altheide and Snow, 1991)

The political strategies of militant groups/action networks are increasingly orientated toward media in their aim to capture the attention of ever-larger audiences. This brings us to another point in the analysis of the visualisation of politics, its dramatistic character. The media increasingly 'frames' political action as political 'spectacles' which have a direct influence on militant groups and their choice of action strategies, encouraging, for example, enactments of violence.

The media spaces opened within media modernity by post-gutenburg technologies are ambiguous in their form. Thompson (1994) argues that mediated publicness is an *open-ended space* in the sense that it is a creative and uncontrollable space, a space where new symbolic forms can be expressed, where new words and images can suddenly appear, where information previously hidden from view can be made available, and where the consequences of becoming visible cannot be fully anticipated and controlled. However, the media are not simply a rosy picture of inherently democratic open-ended spaces of mediated publicness. John Keane (1991) underscores the constraints that media nevertheless pose for mediated political dialogues within its space and Thompson (1994) tempers his analysis of mediated publicness by pointing out that:

> mediated publicness is open-ended in the sense that the contents of mediated materials cannot be entirely delimited in advance — although the degree to which these contents are delimited will depend on the organisation of media institutions and their relations to forms of economic and political power. (p. 246)

Media modernity is a precondition for the contemporary politics of militancy and opens opportunities for militant groups to spread their messages — their symbolic challenges and meaning contestation — beyond the locales of their immediate actions. Not only is the media space opened a precondition for the politics of militancy, but also it seems that in the post-modern world, the media are rapidly becoming the sites of politics itself. The politics of militancy has increasingly moved its terrain of political action to the relatively uncharted virtual territory opened up by Internet. The 1990s have witnessed the advent of a new militant politics in cyberspatial political terrain. 'Cyberwars' — anticipated, threatened or actual — are being fought on Internet.

The media are both a medium, a conduit for the dissemination of meaning *and* actors in the dissemination of meanings. While the media spread political messages, they also represent or frame reality either verbally or visually (primarily iconically) by the invisible social and technological machinery of, for example, television and Internet. (Cf. Manning, 1996) Media spaces are inclusive as well as exclusive and are consequently a field of power relations. Or using the conceptual framework of McKenzie Wark (1997), the media is the vector, the conduit, the trajectory, without beginnings or ends, connecting places and powers together. This underlies the inherently ambiguous nature of media. Media are both medium and actors. (Cf. Carpignono, 1998) The media spaces opened are not only symbolic arenas; they are also economic and political arenas. Media are not just open-ended spaces of opportunities, media modernity even poses constraints upon militant groups/action networks within it, which explains the complicated 'love-hate relationship' contemporary militant groups have with the media. (Peterson and Thörn, 2000) Media intrude upon and even penetrate militant groups/action networks, and conversely, militant groups 'hijack' the media spaces opened in media modernity.

Militant Groups/Action Networks in Media Modernity

The visual media spaces opened by TV and the evening newspapers have created a new situation, which has given smaller and relatively resource 'poor' militant action groups an amplified voice. Through the use of spectacular actions small groups could find a broader public for their messages by manipulating these spaces. In a metaphorical sense they hijack these media spaces in order to spread their messages. This situation is apparent with militant actions staged by small militant action groups in Sweden. However, this situation has also become apparent with the spread of terrorist actions played out within the spatial centralisation of Western cities vulnerable to the violent actions carried out by relatively small groups of activists. Their symbolical messages (which can be directed to a situation across the globe) are immediately spread throughout the 'global' media space. Walter Laqueur (1977) says about 'terrorists' and their relationship to the media that:

> [t]errorists have learned that the media are of paramount importance in their campaign, that the terrorist act itself is next to nothing, whereas publicity is all. But the media, constantly in need of diversity and new angles, make fickle friends. Terrorists will always have to be innovative. They are, in some respects, the super-entertainers of our time. (p. 223)

As Philip Schlesinger (1991) points out, the centrality of the media for contemporary terrorism has become almost a social science truism.

A number of social theorists working on issues concerning international terrorism emphasise terrorists' manipulation of media as they stage their actions.   Brian Jenkins, the Rand Corporation's expert on terrorism, states that: "[t]errorists choreograph their violence. Terrorism is theatre". (Cited in Schlesinger, p. 24) Schlesinger tempers the appeal of this perspective, which sees violence as unambiguously effective drama, or put more strongly, sees the media as "the willing victims of the superstars of violence" (Ibid.), by reminding us that the state in liberal democracies has also developed sophisticated strategies for the management of publicity in connection with subversive acts. I argue, in addition, that this rather one-sided perspective of the media as hapless victims of the publicity strategies of terrorists, or of political protest in general, for that matter, should be further tempered by an understanding of the relative autonomy of the media. Neither terrorists nor the state fully control how the events played out will be framed by media; that is, how the meaning of the actions will be conveyed to the viewing and reading public. The media are not a transparent 'window on the world' — they effect what is happening. This brings us to our discussion of the media as political actors.

Media as Political Actors

Thus far we have looked upon the mediated nature of the politics of militancy. At this point we will turn to a perspective suggested by Paolo Carpignano (1998) and perceive the media as a public sphere. Carpignono argues that:

> the media can be looked at, not simply as a technology of communication, or as an institution that regulates communication, but as, itself, a social relation of communication. (p. 3)

While spectacular actions may readily find exposure in the media, the media's role in 'framing' the action is, of course, essential for how this exposure is received by the viewing or reading public.[1] Along the

---

1 Drawing on the work of Erving Goffman, David Snow and various of his collegues (Snow et al. 1986; Snow and Benford 1988) have developed the concept of "frame alignment processes" to describe the efforts by which social movement organisations

same lines, 'Hickory', an antiracist activist, emphasises the importance of the media for contextualising their militant actions in order that a discussion is initiated regarding their perspectives and tactics in the struggle. Without coverage by the media, on their terms, the political implications of an action are lost. His organisation, *Anti-fascist Action*, in connection with all of their actions, sends out press releases which explain their interpretation of the situation and which explain their choice of action strategy and the goal of their action. In the Syndicalism newspaper, *Arbetaren* (no. 7, 1995.02.17), 'Hickory' expresses his disappointment with the leftist news media which he claims has systematically rejected publishing their press releases and has 'put a lid on' the discussion of a militant struggle against racism and fascism which employs illegal violent tactics. While he can understand that the news media as a whole are reluctant to publish any motivation for sabotage actions, he does not understand the leftist news media's reluctance and what he calls their "intolerant law-abidedness". According to 'Hickory', this is unfortunate as:

> an important purpose of actions today is to iniate discussions, demonstrate different action possibilities and to set the ball in motion, so to say. And it is precisely this process which is obstructed when the actions are kept silent. (Ibid.)

In short, 'Hickory' accuses news media, from the right as well as the left, of a political bias, which condemns all militant struggles as *per se* illegitimate. He argues that media employ a number of strategies to achieve these ends: a strategy of repudiation can be exchanged for a strategy of invisibility, and a strategy of ridicule can be employed interchangeably with a strategy of demonisation. Whatever the strategy or combination of strategies employed, the result is the same — militant political resistance is defined as lying outside of the realm of the legitimate political culture. In this sense, 'Hickory's' analysis is astute, perhaps one of the most fundamental functions of news media, if not the most fundamental function, is their framing of what is regarded as legitimate, respective illegitimate political action. The

---

seek to join their cognitive orientations with potential sympathisers and the public in general. Frame analysis has generated during the last ten years a vast body of scholarship, particularily within the work of American social movement researchers.

media helps establish the 'rules of the political game'. These 'rules of the political game' are of course not fixed, in specific situations even militant illegal actions can be deemed as morally and politically correct, i.e. legitimate. The Swedish media's coverage of the militant protest events surrounding Greenpeace's actions in protest of France's nuclear testing in the Pacific during 1995, which were positively and even heroically portrayed, is an excellent example of the changing nature of political 'rules' and awarded legitimacy. Furthermore, these 'rules' are contested within the media, as the news media itself is not hegemonious. However, news media are integral in the ongoing process of defining a society's political culture.

The mass media does not simply mirror a society's self-understanding. Rather the mass media plays a relatively autonomous role, actively involved in society's self-reflective processes, forming society's self-understanding. The ideological or discursive power of mass media lies in the possibility to define and interpret events and situations. Todd Gitlin (1980) emphasises the ways in which the media 'frames' reality and subsequently influences the media public's perception of reality.[2] Working along the same lines, Stuart Hall (1982) argues that every definition is the subject for struggle and negotiations in order that a collective understanding and support for a particular definition is mobilised. Mass media actively works towards winning this support and legitimacy for a particular definition of a situation or an event by awarding their definition a self-evidence and appealing to the viewing and reading public's 'common sense'. (Cf. Peterson, 1997a) In this way mass media's ideological message is hidden behind a shroud of 'common sense'. In conclusion, media are not only a potential and integral resource for militant groups/action networks. Media can even enter the movement struggles as an identifiable actor. In this sense media actively sets the political agenda.

---

2 Gamson et. al. (1992) warn that media generally operate in ways that promote apathy and quiescence rather than political participation, but they maintain that the "news is not all bad".

> The good news is that the messages provide a many-voiced, open text that can and often is read [the decoding of sights and sounds as well as printed text] oppositionally, at least in part. ... The underdetermined nature of media discourse allows plenty of room for challengers such as social movements to offer competing constructions of reality and to find support for them from readers whose daily lives may lead them to construct meaning in ways that go beyond media imagery. (p. 373)

However the story thus far is not complete, communications networks developed 'underneath' and 'beyond' the structure of state powers and the market control of large-scale media corporations — so-called bush telegraphs — liberate and empower communication channels between individual activists and militant groups and action networks making the politics of militancy. (Cf. Keane, 1991) Through these bush telegraphs — the heteroarchy of communications media — militant 'voices', what Nancy Fraser (1992) calls 'subaltern counterpublics', or what Gitlin (1998) calls "sphericules", are heard which would otherwise be silenced or their meanings distorted by traditional communications media, hence, the necessity for the construction of alternative communications media.

Alternative Media Spaces

Militant groups/action networks develop strategies by which they attempt to 'bypass' mediated publicness, to retreat from its 'gaze'. For example, in the late 1960s the 'new' women's liberation movement self-reflexively constructed a 'free space' in their small conscious-raising group strategy where women could formulate their collective political identity without subjecting themselves to 'the rules of the game' prevailing in mediated publicness. In the 'free space' of the small group women could retreat from the mirror of media societies and 'speak' undisturbed. (Cf. Thörn, 1997) And while a strategy of retreat from media modernity is, and has been, an important source of empowerment for militant groups which rely more or less upon a 'veil of secrecy', the construction of their own media spaces has played an equally important role for their discursive strategies. In other words, bypassing the mediation of commercial, public service and/or state-controlled media on the part of militant groups/action networks does not only take the form of a retreat, they even develop their own 'media spaces' parallel to the media spaces occupied by the established media — by writing and distributing pamphlets, publishing their own newspapers and newsletters, putting up placards, and simply talking to people in schools, at workplaces, and on the streets, as well as the construction of alternative cultural institutions for the distribution of their meaning constructions, e.g. festivals, theatres, activist camps, music and film productions and distributors, etc. These alternative media spaces, both mediated and channels for face-to-face communication, created by militant groups/action networks are essential for spreading their meaning construction in terms which are not subject to the interpretations and 'framing' of the commercial, public service, or state-controlled media.

New alternative media for militant political action are being developed within the framework of the politics of militancy, so-called tactical media that are:

> media of crisis, criticism and opposition. This is both the source of their power, but also their limitation. Their typical heroes are: the activist, the Nomadic media warriors, the pranxter, the hacker, the street rapper, the camcorder kamikaze, they are happy negatives always in search of an enemy. (Lovink, 1997)

The application of new alternative media — tactical media — to militant political action goes beyond established media channels and exists well outside of the realm of parliamentarian or electoral forms of politics. These are media applications that both include and move beyond the discursive and dialogic model of democracy, adding the dimension and confrontational style of direct militant action.

Recent technological developments in electronic media have both widened the potential geographical scope of the alternative media spaces penetrating both the national and transnational public spheres, as well as made their media products cheaper and more sophisticated. These technological innovations have, for example, put cheap camcorders in the hands of militant Swedish animal rights activists and made available the sophisticated layout and graphic design computer techniques which have been put at the disposal of the activist editors of racist and fascist periodicals in Sweden. But perhaps the most spectacular development, in regards to the alternative media spaces being opened by contemporary militant groups/action networks, has been the Internet which has become both a prime channel of mediated communication for militant action networks, as well as a cyber terrain for direct political action. Militant activists are travelling on the 'information highway' more and more, making use of electronic delivery systems:

1. in order to reach out to potentially new supporters;
2. in order to co-ordinate political actions across ever wider territorial action spaces of political militancy;

3. in order to establish 'discussion groups' — new forms of community — which are constructed on the Net and the internal cohesion and collective identity of the militant action network is maintained in this way; and, perhaps most importantly, making Internet — cyberspace;
4. as a site or virtual terrain for militant political struggle.

In the remaining pages we will deal with these four aspects of cyberspace for the politics of political militancy.

Information Dissemination and Action Co-ordination on Internet.

A Web home-page is an information outlet for an ideal, commercial, or governmental organisation/group or individual. For example, in 1996 Swedish *Nordland* (a neo-nazi network which produces a magazine, a CD company, is a White Power concert organiser, and a mail-order outlet) set up a sophisticated home-page on Internet's World Wide Web where they offer news, ideological texts, and links to the home pages of kindred groups. On the page they offer the option to trial-listen excerpts from music recordings in the form of sound files transferred over the Internet. Bjørgo (1997) notes the close ties between *Nordland* and its American counterpart the *Resistance* home-page, which shows that in a breakdown of its statistics of users accessing this home-page the Scandinavian countries occupied three of the top five spots (Sweden second after USA). Bjørgo argues that this is a good indication as to the extent to which Scandinavian racists/nationalist are active on the Internet. According to Bjørgo:

> [a]lthough many of those who log on to such a home page are most likely to be established activists or sympathisers, a considerable proportion are probably curious youths who would hardly have come in contact with a racial revolutionary movement unless it had been only a mouse-click away. Thus, Internet offers a new and fertile arena for both maintaining international networks of activists, and reaching potential recruits and customers. (pp. 144-145)

Bjørgo claims that in general racial revolutionaries are increasingly using the electronic mediation of their messages made available in cyberspace. These groups are using electronic bulletin boards more and more and especially the Internet to disseminate their ideology and recruit new activists. The establishment of home-pages in World Wide Web by every 'self-respecting' ultra-right group and organisation has meant that it is easy to reach curious and potentially interested persons. Today there are between 50 and 60 Swedish racist home-pages on the Internet and their numbers are growing. According to Torbjörn Ekblom from the Swedish Secret Service, these home-pages on the Internet serve to distribute their racist propaganda, recruit new supporters, communicate with like-minded both in Sweden and increasingly internationally, and lastly, to market their products, e.g. tee-shirts, music and publications. (*Göteborgs Posten* 98.01.16)

According to Bjørgo, for the activists themselves, the Internet offers a potentially effective and risk-free arena for their political activism. Instead of risking a beating at the hands of antiracist activists when they distribute racist flyers on the streets, they distribute these messages unthreatened on the Net. Furthermore, he argues that:

> due to the practical and legal difficulties of policing a borderless cyberspace, it provides (anonymous) extremists with the opportunity to distribute material — including Nazi propaganda and instructions for making bombs — which it would be illegal to disseminate in their own country. (p. 257)

Thus, a new breed of activist has appeared in cyberspace — the Net Nazi. Bjørgo claims that:

> [b]ecause of the borderless nature of the Internet, this technology clearly contributes to one of the most significant trends within the far right in the 1990s — the transformation of traditional chauvinist nationalism into a transnational community of 'racial nationalists'. (Ibid.)

While militant groups/action networks on the far right in Sweden, and Scandinavia in general, have proved themselves adept at exploiting the potential of Internet for the dissemination of their messages, groups and networks on the left have been slower at making use of the 'information highway' provided by Internet. As one antiracist activist pointed out:

> [w]e just don't have the economic resources at hand that the racist and fascist groups have at their disposal. It costs a lot to create an attractive home-page that catches the attention of young people. We don't have that kind of money and we don't really have that sort of know-how either.

Flashback, an Internet home-page started in Sweden by Jan Axelsson, offers multifarious links to 'underground' groups and organisations ranging from ultra-right neo-fascist groups to ultra-left anarchist groups, from paedophile organisations to Satanist groups and networks, under the watchword that information must be freely accessible and that all underground groups, in that they challenge and provoke the establishment, are *per definition* good. *Flashback* is one of the most visited sites in Sweden and their electronic newsletter, *Frihetsbrevet,* is sent out to more than 40,000 subscribers. Statistics over what their visitors link into reveal their interests. While the 'sex links' receive approximately ten times as many visitors as the other links found on the page, among the political links, the fascist home-pages are accessed twice as often as the anarchist home-pages, however, the anarchist sites are accessed more than three times as often as all of the home-pages of the established political parties combined. (*Göteborgs Posten.* 1997.10.05)

While militant groups on the far right in Sweden were early to exploit the potential of Internet, militant groups and networks on the left have nevertheless begun to pick up the slack. However, their efforts to date to create Internet home-pages have been far more amateurish, partly because of their lack of economic resources and know-how and partly because groups on the 'far left' have not had the same ambition as their counterparts on the 'far right', that is, to reach as many potential supporters as possible. According to the activist cited above,

> Anarchists, AFA and other extreme groups don't care if they reach uninitiated. Their pages are just for themselves and others like them. They could care less if they could find new activists through Internet. The fascist groups, on the other hand, design their pages so as to reach out to curious young people, they recruit their followers with these pages.

Nevertheless, militant groups and action networks on the left are rapidly cutting in the slack and are more and more turning to the Internet to decimate their messages and to recruit new followers.

In regards to co-ordination of militant actions, the Internet has proved to be a less viable alternative to face-to-face communication. As we saw in the previous chapter the demand for secrecy, an inevitable element for the successful implementation of a high-risk militant action cannot be met on the Internet. Both secret service agencies and the police closely monitor the Internet channels of political militants. While militant activists attempt to circumvent this cyber-surveillance with the employment of anonymous e-mail addresses, coded messages, etc., it is not their preferred channel for the action co-ordination of a high-risk event. So while the convenience of Internet is recognised for the flow of information and action co-ordination in a 'virtual' transnational and national campaign, other forms of communication are recommended for 'real world' high-risk militant action.

Virtual Communities and Virtual Sects on Internet

BBs (Bulletin Boards), and now Internet, with home-pages and Usenet newsgroups, offers forms for interactive textual relations for individuals to meet both opponents and like-minded. These discussion groups of like-minded subsequently offer these activists new forms of community, which can link activists across wide geographical distances. Discussion groups may be either open (this is a question of more or less open), in which case the 'engaged exclusivity' of traditional political groups and organisations becomes 'ephemeral inclusiveness' (Lemos, 1996), widening its symbolic territory to construct, for example, a transnational cybercommunity of 'racial nationalists', or closed, cementing a specific group in its electronically mediated identity construction as a 'virtual sect' while, at the same time, (potentially) constructing this discursive exclusive cybercommunity over vast geographical distances.

Secret Societies in Cyberspace. The intense group cohesion of the secret society has been classically achieved through face-to-face interactions. Activists and their ongoing discussions have been confined in the 'real world' of place. Internet has opened a new non-physical space for the intensive interactions of secret societies, *sic* neo-sects — cyberspace. Instead of communicating secrets verbally, as is the case for secret societies in their classical sense, the secrets are communicated through the written word. Writing, however, is a visible vehicle for communication. And according to Simmel (1950), "writing possesses an objective existence which renounces all guarantees of remaining secret". (p. 352) For the establishment of secret societies on the Internet, 'virtual sects', a precondition has been the development of methods which assure (more or less) the secrecy of the written word and the anonymity of its authors in cyberspace.

Generally, identity is an amorphous and almost non-existent concept on the Internet for a variety of reasons. One is the inherent fluidity of cyberspace where people emerge and submerge frequently, and absences are not readily noted in the 'community'. Most people remember faces and voices, the primary means of causal identification in the 'real world'. The arbitrary and cryptic sequences of letters and digits comprising e-mail addresses are not particularly noticeable or memorable and far from a unique identification of an individual. Individual identity is unstable and relatively anonymous, and the technology also makes possible relatively anonymous, secret interactions between these anonymous individual identities. From the charter of the cypherpunk mailing list:

> Cypherpunks assume privacy is a good thing and wish there was more of it. Cypherpunks acknowledge that those who want privacy must create it for themselves and not expect governments, corporations, or other large, faceless organisations to grant them privacy out of beneficence. Cypherpunks know that people have been creating their own privacy for centuries with whispers, envelopes, closed doors, and couriers. Cypherpunks do not seek to prevent other people from speaking about their experiences or their opinions. (soda.berkeley.edu:/pub/cypherpunks)

Within the last ten years various techniques have been developed to assure anonymity, for example, encryption and steganography. For steganographic communications in the electronic realm mailing lists are set up where individual messages are broadcasted to the entire list and individual users decode particular messages with their unique key. Unwanted visitors to a secret site on the Internet are excluded through moderation, techniques such as the 'fire extinguisher' and the 'group bouncer' are used to 'squelch' intruders. Originally anonymous posting services were introduced for individual, particularly volatile newsgroups, where anonymity is the preferred method of communication, such as talk.abortion and alt.sex.bondage, which was one of the first, started in 1988. In short, techniques and software are being developed in general to help bring some sort of order within the inevitable chaos which the very surfeit of knowledge and information generated within cyberspace leads towards. For example, information navigating devices like HyperCard@, Gopher, Veronica, and Mosaic are efforts to control the disorder created by the veritable deluge of information confronting us on the Internet. And just as we are inundated by information, the potential number of social connections impinging on us inundates us. Today there is a wide range of closed Internet sites for political groups from the far right to the far left. The creation of closed, or heavily moderated, Usenet newsgroup sites and Internet home-pages is one way of bringing under control the flood of potential social connections available on Internet which directly limits the size and membership of the virtual community formed, constructing what I term the virtual sect. The virtual sect bypasses what Lemos (1996) calls 'ephemeral inclusiveness', the form of virtual community otherwise found in, for example, un-moderated or 'lightly' moderated Usenet newsgroups or Internet home-pages, to create what one could call an 'ephemeral exclusiveness'.

One example of a virtual sect is *Rednet*, a joint debate forum on Internet, which gathers activists from revolutionary groups on the far-left in Sweden. In their programme declaration they state that:

> the aim is to spread information, as well as discuss theoretical, ideological, and practical activism. This is our own forum where we can develop our analysis *without interference* from liberals, bourgeoisie, sexists or racists.

Rednet is a closed discussion group — a retreat from media modernity. In order to gain entry, one has to know someone else in the discussion group. Less that a thousand activists have access to the site and approximately 70 or so actively participate within the 25 different ongoing secret discussions. In order to keep the number of contributions to the discussions within a reasonable level the number of participants must be kept in turn at a 'reasonable' level. In short, these are small groups and the 'codes' or 'rules' for participation are strict. The innovation is quite simply that physical presence is no longer a necessary precondition for the interactive relations which underlie the strong sense of exclusivity or 'we' which welds the secret discussion groups, *sic* neo-sects, together. Their collective identity is electronically mediated; hence their identity is 'virtual'.

Cybercommunities of 'Ephemeral Inclusiveness'. While the older technique of Bulletin Board stations was always more or less closed in that one had to first have access to the telephone number of the station in order to connect to the link, as well as being a costly technique for activists who wished to go online and interact with activists internationally; Internet offers an entirely new potential for cheap, and relatively open 'places' for interaction between militant activists and potential supporters, partly through World Wide Web home-pages, which appear to be the preferred channel for militant activists in Sweden and the rest of Europe, and partly through Usenet newsgroups which are more often used by activists in USA.

Firstly, an important qualification regarding the openness of these Internet sites for cybercommunities of 'ephemeral inclusiveness' is that they are *relatively open*. All of these sites, whether they are home-pages or newsgroups, are more or less moderated. The 'owner' of the home-page or the appointed moderator of the newsgroup is responsible for what messages are relayed. They may more or less vigorously weed out unwanted interventions in the discussions. For example, the owner of an antiracist home-page may very well exclude a bombardment of racist interventions on his/her page. So not only does the home-page owner or newsgroup moderator determine how long the interactions will appear textually in cyberspace, but they also determine, more or less, what and who will appear textually in cyberspace. In short, 'ephemeral inclusiveness' is a somewhat overly exaggerated notion of the quality of the communities tentatively under construction within cyberspace.

Furthermore, the authors on these Internet pages not only formulate their own messages; they recycle and counterpoise their opponents' messages within a new frame of reference. For example, on neo-fascist pages one can find both extensive and up-to-date information regarding antifascist groups and organisations, links to their pages and even names and addresses of their key activists. For example, during January 1998 a nazi organisation calling itself 'anti-afa' published on their Internet home-page the names, addresses, pictures and other information (e.g. active member of a communist youth organisation, 'nigger', 'vegan', 'homosexual', etc.) regarding ten militant antiracist activists in Helsingborg, a small city on the south coast of Sweden, and now the list is growing, including militant antiracist activists throughout the country. They claim that their list is a direct response to a similar list that has appeared on the home-page of Antifascist Action in Halmstad. On this list a handful of fascist activists were named together with a message that Nazis were being watched and if they should appear on the streets with their symbols or threaten anyone, then "we (the antifascist youth) will take hard measures". (*Göteborgs Posten* 98.01.16) For these groups, their battle is more and more being conducted in cyberspace. In this way, by counterpoising their antagonists electronic messages, they usurp the messages of antiracists, providing them with a new context and subsequently lending them new meanings in a form of, to paraphrase Umberto Eco, 'semiotic guerrilla warfare'. On an antiracist group's home-page it is not uncommon that racist and neo-fascist cyber activists intervene in the discussions. In short, on these Internet pages a digital war is fought out in cyberspace between antagonists in a discursive struggle.

Secondly, it is difficult to assess the quality of the interactive sense of 'we', if there is a sense of collective identity at all, being formed on the Internet. Relatively open home-pages or newsgroups, which include interactions between like-minded as well as opponents, perhaps more resemble the heated exchanges between parts in a dispute in the letters to the editor pages of daily newspapers than they resemble the interactions of face-to-face communities of militant activists. And thirdly, the exchanges between like-minded may very well reinforce a sense of we, a sense of community, but how lasting this sense of community is would appear to be highly tentative and, lastly, these digital interactions do not guarantee that this sense of community in cyberspace will result in the concerted real world actions of its participants.

Internet as a transmitter of information has become a vital tool for: the maintenance of militant activist networks; militant action co-ordination across vast geographical distances; and, the recruitment of new supporters for militant groups/action networks. These are, perhaps, the most important functions of the Internet for these groups and networks. However, transcending this transmission of information, Internet, in addition, offers a space for the *ritual sharing* of information which binds communities in cyberspace. Militant groups/action networks, with the opening of cyber 'places', are constructing their collective identities in new ways, subverting time, and most importantly distance, to create both virtual communities of activists, as well as virtual sects which are both formed at a distance via ties to what Lemos (1996) has called a symbolic empathic proximity.

*From the Paris Salon to the Boston Tea Party: Cybersites of Militant
Political Struggle*

What we have discussed thus far is the Internet as a channel for
rhetorical militant resistance. That is, militant resistance which focuses
upon the content of Internet communication; Internet as a
communication media, as a tool to exchange text, images, and sound,
and where the two primary means of militant Internet communication
are through the use of e-mail and through the World Wide Web. It is
the content of the messages which makes this kind of Internet usage
militant, i.e. whether the message content contributes to an escalation
of enactments of violence, potential, threatened or actual (real or virtual)
in the political struggle. The messages can be sent among militant
cyber activists or they can be sent from militant activists to opponents.
Militant messages sent from militant cyber activists to opponents
(many-to-one; many-to few) normally take the shape of denunciatory
protest messages threatening some form of real or virtual retaliation
for a policy or action. Militant messages among cyber activists (one-
to-one; one-to-few; one-to-many; few-to-many) can consist of a variety
of types, e.g. personal notes, discussions, proposals for militant actions,
announcements of militant campaigns, etc.

But perhaps more radically another kind of militant Internet usage
challenges the relations of power in the political cyberspaces opened
by Internet, that is, technical resistance which centres on the form of
Internet communication — the infrastructure of the Internet. This
typology of militant Internet usage extends the avenues of militancy,
offering new virtual sites or targets for direct militant resistance, where
militant actions are directed against the very superstructure of the
Internet.

Stefan Wray (1998a), has argued that today's cyber cultures and
cyber politics are biased toward the more discursive and dialogic
Habermasian "Paris Salon model" of electronic democracy and that
the more active and direct "Boston Tea Party model" of electronic
democracy is largely ignored by more 'legitimate' actors and
communication theorists alike. Nevertheless, a new form of militant
political activism is emerging in the latter 1990s which, while it does
not deny the validity of the new forms of political communication
taking form on the Internet, is propagating for an extension of the
dialogic forms of democracy to include more luddite forms of direct

virtual activism. They are moving electronic democracy from being defined within the confines of political communication (debate, discussion, dialogue) discussed above and widening the frame to include also extra-parliamentarian, non-electoral forms of direct action. Nothing new for political protest in general, which have always hosted, together with reasoned dialogue in the public sphere, or in the succinct terms of Todd Gitlin (1998), political communication within "sphericules", these forms of political activity — ranging from mass rallies and demonstrations, sit-ins, pickets, occupations and blockades, to civil unrest, riots, and even sabotage. The new is rather that the sites for these militant actions are moved from the 'real world' to the virtual world of Internet. The Internet infrastructure itself is increasingly becoming a site or target for militant political action. Internet is increasingly hosting cyberspatial Boston Tea Parties, where, instead of dumping tea to protest the policies of an imperial power, cyber activists are dumping data or engaging in other forms of direct action on the Internet. (Cf. Wray, 1998a)

The Critical Art Ensemble, a New York based cyber activist group, has published two books (1994 and 1996) which sketch the theory and practice of the new emerging militant cyber activism. Departing from a theoretical understanding as to the changing nature of power relations and their locations, which builds upon the earlier work of Hakim Bey (1991), they argue that power has become fluid, mobile, dispersed and nomadic. They argue that earlier sedimentary forms of power are being replaced by nomadic forms of power which are electronically constituted. "The locations of power — and the site of resistance — rest in an ambiguous zone without borders". (Critical Art Ensemble, 1994: 11) Subsequently, any resistance to power must take this fluidity, mobility, dispersion, and nomadism into consideration. That is, effective resistance must mirror these attributes, which is best done in the cyberspatial political territories of Internet:

> Nomadic power must be resisted in cyberspace rather than in physical space. A small but co-ordinated group of hackers could introduce electronic viruses, worms, and bombs into the data banks, programs, and networks of authority, possibly bringing the destructive force of inertia into the nomadic realm. Prolonged inertia equals the collapse of nomadic authority on a global level. Such a strategy does not require action in numerous geographic areas. (Ibid. 25)

The Critical Art Ensemble (1996) describe their theory of militant cyber resistance as part of a continuum to 'earlier' real world social movements:

> The strategy and tactics of Electronic Civil Disobedience should not be a mystery to any activists. They are the same as traditional civil disobedience. Electronic Civil Disobedience is a non-violent activity by its very nature, since the oppositional forces never physically confront one another. As in civil disobedience, the primary tactics in Electronic Civil Disobedience are trespass and blocking. The contestational force must occupy exits, entrances, conduits, and other key spaces in order to bring pressure on legitimised institutions engaged in unethical or criminal actions. Blocking information conduits is analogous to blocking physical locations; however, electronic blockages can cause financial stress that physical blockage cannot, and it can be used beyond the local level. Electronic Civil Disobedience is civil disobedience reinvigorated. What civil disobedience once was, Electronic Civil Disobedience is now. (p. 18)

Inspired by the political theory of Gilles Deleuze and Felix Guattari in their seminal work *A Thousand Plateaus* (1987 [1980]), Stefan Wray (1998b) argues that a resistant e-mail message travelling through the Internet follows "non-linear rhizomatic-nomadic pathways". (p. 16) The 'rhizomatic-nomadic' militant e-mail moves from one person to another individually, as part of a larger cc: list, or via a listserve. This militant message is then copied and redistributed. This process continues to reproduce itself. An original sender cannot know where and when the militant message stops travelling, stops being copied and redistributed, stops being translated. Furthermore, militant texts, images, and sounds on web sites are often linked hyper-textually with similar sites. A reader, user, an audience member of a militant web site can connect easily to another such site and in this way can, according to Wray, "rhizomatically and nomadically travel through a territory of cyberspace" (Ibid.) that has been occupied by a series of interconnected militant web sites. Given the multitude of possible pathways leading a militant activist user from one web site to another, the militant activist in this case can be said to wander nomadically through the particular militant territorium.

These kinds of militant Internet use, technical militant resistance, centres on the form of Internet communication and construct the Internet infrastructure as a site for militant acts. So far these militant cyberactions have mainly borrowed the notions of trespass and blockade from traditional civil disobedience tactics and applied these tactics to the Internet infrastructure, blockading or jamming up web sites of political opponents. Preventing so-called legitimate usage has been the preferred practice of what has become more widely known as Electronic Civil Disobedience. Proponents of Electronic Civil Disobedience concede that the tactics of, for example, a virtual sit-in perhaps will not force authorities to change their policies, but rather the protest tactic is designed to create a form of electronic theatre that indirectly increases solidarity among activists and propagates a political message to 'other layers' of the Internet. (Kaplan, 1999) These forms of militant cyberactivism, somewhere between a digital sit-in and 'cybotage', appear to be defining themselves as treading ground between disruption and destruction. However, according to David Ronfeldt at the Rand Corporation, "[c]onflict in the information age will be more about disruption than destruction. And much of the disruption will be symbolic even if it is aggressive". (cited in Kaplan, 1999: 39)

Militant actions upon the infrastructure of the Internet stage, enactments of violent resistance upon sites of entry — pathways leading toward, and entranceways to — opponents' computer systems. These sites can be overloaded, clogged, and finally blocked to create an electronic disturbance for an opponent. E-mail based militant acts of resistance move beyond e-mail use for the transmission of resistant political messages, i.e. sending messages of dissent to a political opponent. An overabundance of e-mails filling an opponent's inbox with thousands of unwanted messages can cause the ISP server to crash. When such spaming of e-mail reaches these proportions an e-mail bomb is said to have been employed. In the same way that massive e-mail sent to an e-mail address blocks those paths and entrances, a massive assault on the entranceways to a web site can cause blockage. An electronic pulse system can be established that sends repeated requests for entry to a single web site asking that particular site to respond and load itself upon the resistant actors' net browser. Militant cyberactivists have designed software programmes that automate this repeated pressing the net browser's 'reload' button. Hence, acting in concert with other militant cyberactivists in a distributed system, such action can cause an overflow of reload requests that prevents others from accessing the targeted site. The first software programmes developed to automate the action of repeated simultaneous multiple key striking have been called 'ping engines', relatively small and unsophisticated programmes. Another engine is the offshore spam engine, a form-driven website based in another country that enables a user to automatically distribute massive quantities of e-mail to particular e-mail addresses. However, once a targeted e-mail address becomes self aware of an e-mail onslaught, their cyber security teams can put up barriers. These programmes are becoming progressively more sophisticated and as rapidly as governments and corporations are developing counter-measures to these programmes, cyber activists are in turn developing new and better Electronic Civil Disobedience devices. [3]

The Electronic Disturbance Theatre, a small group of cyber activists and artists engaged in developing the theory and practice of Electronic Civil Disobedience, working at the intersections of radical militant politics, recombinant and performance art, and computer software design, has developed an engine called Flood Net, a URL based software used to flood and block entry to an opponent's web site. In the planning stages is a proposal for the development of a SWARM, i.e. an array of Flood Net-like devices, arising, acting, and dispersing simultaneously against an array of cyberspatial political targets:

> If the electronic pulses generated by our Flood Net actions are represented by a small mountain stream, the electronic pulses generated by a swarm of convergent Electronic Civil Disobedience actions are a raging torrent. (http://www.thing.net/-rdom/ecd/EDTECD.html)

---

3 This is a relatively new dimension of conflict which has mobilised considerable theoretical, as well as technical, resources. According to a recent report from the California based think-tank, the Rand Corporation, entitled *In Athena's Camp: Preparing for Conflict in the Information Age,* authors John Arguilla and David Ronfeldt define infowar, or cyberwar, as "conducting military operations according to information-related principles. ... It means disrupting or destroying information and communications systems". (http://www.flora.org/flora.comnet-www/1337) According to Gregory Waters, the world of information warfare is:

> a world where logic bombs, computer viruses, trojan-horses, precision-guided munitions, stealth designs, radio-electronic combat systems, new electronics for intelligence gathering and deception, microwave weapons, space-based weapons, and robotic warfare are being discussed, developed and deployed. (Ibid.)

So if militant 'hacktivists' are tuning their weapons for the struggle, no less are the authorities preparing themselves for this new kind of political warfare. Research into this aspect of the intersection between communications, political action, and the Internet is thickly peopled by representatives from security intelligence services, the military establishment, various private sector security-related companies, and select academics.

Taking the cyber politics of militancy one step further, or one level deeper if you will, are militant actions which do not stop at the entranceways to opponent's computer systems, but that enter the very interior of the system. In these cases militant 'hacktivists' trespass upon the interior of an opponent's system in order to destroy, remove, or corrupt data. Obviously, this 'deep-level' form of cyber militancy is both the most difficult, requiring the advanced skills of computer programmers, as well as the most high-risk, i.e. entail the greatest degree of danger for legal prosecution. Meeting the requirements for advanced skills a new breed of cyber activists has emerged in the 1990s, the so-called 'hacktivist', the politised computer hacker. This convergence of the computerised activist and the politicised hacker, a hybridised activist-hacker, opens up unforeseen doors and possibilities in the militant politics of cyberspace.   Lending their expertise to cyberpolitics, the level of militancy, i.e. the degree of disruption and ultimately destruction of targeted sites within the political terrain of Internet, has been dramatically enhanced. Questions of legality emerge with the application of more sophisticated techniques of cyber disruption.   In general, the higher one is on the tactical scale, i.e. the deeper the militant cyber activist probes in the opponent's computer system, the higher the risk.   Hence, the more crucial it is for the 'hacktivists' to mask their identities and not to leave traces of their militant actions. Having several different free e-mail accounts under assumed names is one way militant cyber activists accomplish this goal.   A number of web sites now offer free e-mail accounts where anonymity is possible.

The types of these militant actions of disruption, and even destruction, vary. An individual 'hacktivist' or group of cyber activists can change the content of an opponent's web site, removing, adding or changing images and text. This is analogous to billboard alteration or other print-based types of cultural jamming. An article in the *Ottawa Citizen* (1998.10.25) reports on the action of Milworm, acting together with the group Ashtray Lumberjacks, which orchestrated an unprecedented mass hack of more than 300 sites around the world, replacing Web pages with an anti-nuclear statement — complete with angry red mushroom clouds — directed towards all of the nuclear powers. Also during 1998, the Portuguese group Kaotik Team hacked 45 Indonesian government Websites, altering Web pages to include messages calling for full autonomy for East Timor. (Ibid.) In a sense the Internet becomes a vast, high profile canvas for political graffiti, where cyber activists enter web sites to erase, add, or change information. Furthermore, 'hacktivists' can launch a corrupted intelligent into a web site. For example, 'hacktivists', or deep programmers, are now developing intelligent agents that can crawl through a web site. A certain type of intelligent agent is called a spider. 'Good spiders' are designed to crawl quickly though web sites in search of pertinent information. While 'bad spiders' are being designed to crawl very slowly with the intent of causing a disruption.

Militant Swedish activists, perhaps the most densely online militant action groups/networks in the world, have been quick to employ the possibilities opened by Internet. The 'Day of Net Attacking against Vivisection', part of the wider 'Operation Close Down', is a campaign started by the Swedish Animal Liberation Front against SMI (Smittskyddsinstitutet, a vivisection institute in Stockholm) and the experiments conducted there. This action, carried out on January 15, 1999, was the first ever animal liberation Electronic Civil Disobedience action. In co-operation with the Tactical Internet Response Network web site which made available Flood Net to cyber animal rights activists, over 800 people from 15 countries participated. The staged global virtual sit-in was deemed by its organisers as a success. One hour into the action SMI held a national press conference and announced that they had decided to pull their entire computer network off the Internet for days. Furthermore, the organisers announced that the action and the issue of vivisection were reported widely in Swedish and Italian main stream media, who emphasise the hybridised forms militant actions, assume. (http://www.animal-liberation.net/tactical/) A virtual action is made 'real' when it obtains visibility in conventional media.

Again emphasising the hybridised nature of the 'new' politics of militancy, in February 1999 activists from the United States and Canada held demonstrations at the Seattle Fur Exchange while over 1,000 cyber activists from around the world participated in a global virtual sit-in at the Seattle Fur Exchange's web site via the Flood Net device. The Seattle Fur Exchange pulled the entire cybercast of their auction and sales prices for pelts were reported as dismal. The success of this action prompted a similar action in March of that year at the Finnish Fur Sales web site. (frontline@rocketmail.com)

Wray (1998a) argues that the kinds of Internet direct actions that have taken place so far, especially those that attempt to involve mass participation as opposed to the more solitary attacks of the lone hacker, seem to still be in an early stage of development. What we are mostly seeing are experiments. Wray wrote this evaluation in the autumn of 1998. While writing now in 1999 I would agree with the basic premises, that virtual mass participation in militant cyber actions is still in its experimental stage, the experiments have come a long way indeed in a very short time. Virtual sit-ins have rapidly become an everyday occurrence, using increasingly sophisticated civil disobedience devices, in the action repertoires of militant groups/action networks.

The Politics of Militancy in Media Modernity

Guy Debord (1971 and 1990) argues that the spectacle is not a collection of images, but a social relation among people, mediated by images. The mediated publicness of media modernity makes visible the spectacles, or in Debord's terms, is a pure spectacle', which while militant groups cannot escape its totalising effects, can, nevertheless, engage with it — embrace it, appropriate it, speak its language, use its images, throw its trash cans as the Punks do, explode it — in short, engage with the society to which the spectacle gives expression in various ways. And in doing so, militant groups in the politics of visibility opened by media modernity make opaque the power relations within the questions they are addressing. Furthermore, militant cyber activists are embracing the new terrain of politics opened by contemporary electronic media, confronting the fluid, nomadic relations of power in cyberspace — throwing its virtual trashcans — with a militant resistance of virtual 'nomadic hordes' of 'hacktivists'. Engaging with relations of power which are constituted electronically on the Internet, as well as in direct actions in the 'real' world, cyber activists may very well be ushering in a new revitalised phase of the politics of militancy. While the streets will not be depopulated by militant activists, nor will mass media discontinue to be a target arena for militant politics in search of publicness, we are likely to see a proliferation of hybridised actions that involve a multiplicity of militant tactics combining actions on the street and actions in cyberspace.

Bibliography

Abrahams, Roger (1981) 'Shouting Match at the Border: The Folklore of Display Events' in R. Bauman and R. Abrahams (eds.) *"And Other Neighbourly Names". Social Processes and Cultural Image in Texas Folklore.* Austin: University of Texas Press.

Alberoni, Francesco (1984) *Movement and Institution.* New York: Columbia University Press.

Altheide, David and Snow, Robert (1991) *Media Worlds in the Era of Postjournalism.* New York: Aldine de Gruyter.

Bauman, Zygmunt (1999) *Culture as Praxis.* London: Sage.

Bauman, Zygmunt (1993) 'Racism, Antiracism and Moral Progress', stencil, Leeds.

Beck, Ulrich (1997) *The Reinvention of Politics.* Cambridge: Polity Press.

Becker, Howard (1946) *German Youth: Bond or Free.* London: Kegan Paul, Trench, Trubner & Co., LTD.

Bellman, Beryl (1984) *The Language of Secrecy: Symbols and Metaphors in Poro Ritual.* New Brunswick, New Jersey: Rutgers University Press.

Benedikt, Michael (1991) 'Cyberspace. Some Proposals', in M. Benedikt (ed.), *Cyberspace.* Cambridge: MIT Press.

Bey, Hakim (1991) *T.A.Z. The Temporary Autonomous Zone, Ontological Anarchy, Poetic Terrorism.* Brooklyn, NY: Autonomedia.

Bhabha, Homi (1990) 'Introduction: Narrating the Nation' in H. Bhabha (ed.) *Nation and Narration.* London and New York: Routledge.

Bjørgo, Tore (1997) *Racist and Right-Wing Violence in Scndinavia.* Doctoral dissertation submitted to the University of Leiden.

Brottslighet kopplad till rikets inre säkerhet under 1997. (1998) report from Rikspolisstyrelsen Säkerhetspolisen. Stockhom.

Brottslighet kopplad till rikets inre säkerhet under 1995/1996. (1997) report from Rikspolisstyrelsen Säkerhetspolisen. Stockhom.

Brottslighet kopplad till rikets inre säkerhet under 1994 och 1995. (1996) report from Rikspolisstyrelsen Säkerhetspolisen. Stockhom.

Burke, Kenneth (1945) *Grammar of Motives,* Englewood Cliffs, N.J.: Prentice Hall.

Butler, Judith (1997) *Excitable Speech: A Politics of the Performative.* New York and London: Routledge.

Canetti, Elias (1960) *Masse und Macht.* Düsseldorf: Claassen Verlag.

Clarke, John et al. (1976) 'Sub-cultures, cultures and class: a theoretical overview' in S. Hall and T. Jefferson (eds.) *Resistance Through Rituals: Youth Sub-cultures in Post-war Britian.* London: Hutchinson.

Cohen, Erik (1983) 'The Structural Transformation of the Kibbutz' in Ernest Krausz (ed.) *The Sociology of the Kibbutz. Volume II.* New Brunswick (USA): Transaction Books.

Cohen, Jean L. and Arato, Andrew (1996) 'The Public Sphere, The Media and Civil Society' in A. Sajo (ed.) *Rights of Access to the Media.* Amsterdam: Kluwer Law International.

168   *Contemporary Political Protest*

Cohen, Jean L. and Arato, Andrew (1992) *Civil Society and Political Theory*. Cambridge: MIT Press.
Cooley, Charles (1956) *The Two Major Works of Charles H. Cooley*. Glencoe, Ill.: University of Chicago Press.
Critical Art Ensemble (1996) *Electronic Civil Disobedience and Other Unpopular Ideas*. Brooklyn: Autonomedia.
Critical Art Ensemble (1994) *The Electronic Disturbance*. Brooklyn: Autonomedia.
Davis, Fei-Ling (1971) *Primitive Revolutionaries of China: A Study of Secret Societies in the Late Nineteenth Century*. London and Henley: Routledge and Kegan Paul.
Debord, Guy (1990) *Comments on the Society of the Spectacle*. London: Verso.
de Certeau, M. (1984) *The Practice of Everyday Life*. London and Berkeley: University of California Press.
Debord, Guy (1971) *La société du spectacle: la théorie situationniste*. Paris: Champ libre.
Deleuze, Gilles and Guattari (1987) *A Thousand Plateaus*. Minneapolis: University of Minneasota Press.
della Porta, Donatello (1995) *Social movements, political violence, and the state: A comparative analysis of Italy and Germany*. New York: Cambridge University Press.
Derrida, Jaques (1997) *The Politics of Friendship*. London and New York: Verso.
Docherty, Brian (1996) 'Paving the Way: The Rise of Direct Action Against Roadbuilding and the Changing Character of British Environmentalism', *Keele Research Paper*. no. 21. Keele University: Department of Politics.
Douglas, Mary (1973) *The Idea of Purity in Ancient Judaism*. Leiden: Brill.
Douglas, Mary (1970) *Natural Symbols: explorations in cosmology*. London: Barrie & Rockliff.
Durkheim, Émile (1965) *The Elementary Forms of the Religious Life*. New York: Free Press.
Eco, Umberto (1995) 'Unlimited Semeiosis and Drift: Pragmaticism vs. *Pragmaticism"* in Kenneth Laine Kettner (ed.) *Peirce and Contemporary Thought*. New York: Fordham University Press.
Eco, Umberto (1984) *Semiotics and the Philosophy of Language*. London: Macmillan Press.
Emirbayer, Mustafa (1996) 'Useful Durkheim', *Sociological Theory*. 14 (2).
Enzenberger, Hans Magnus (1993) *Inbördes Krig*. Stockholm: Nordstedts.
Esherick, Joseph and Wasserstrom, Jeffrey (1990) 'Acting Out Democracy: Political Theater in Modern China', *The Journal of Asien Studies*. 49 (4).
Evreinoff, Nicolas (1927) *The Theatre in Life*. New York: Benjamin Bloom.
Eyerman, Ron (1996) 'Sociala rörelsers kulturella praxis', *Sociologisk forskning*,(1).
Eyerman, Ron (1994) *Between Culture and Politics: Intellectuals in Modern Society*. Oxford: Polity Press.
Eyerman Ron and Jamison, Andrew (1998) *Music and Social Movements: Mobilizing Traditions in the Twentieth Century*. New York and Cambridge: Cambridge University Press.
Eyerman, Ron and Jamison, Andrew (1991) *Social Movements: A Cognitive Approach*. Cambridge: Polity Press.
Feldman, Allen (1991) *Formations of Violence: The Narrtives of the Body and Political Terror in Northern Ireland*. Chicago and London: University of Chicago Press.
Flacks, Richard (1988) *Making History: The American Left and the American Mind*. New York: Columbia University Press.
Fong, Mak Lau (1981) *The Sociology of Secret Societies: A Study of Chinese Secret Societies in Singapore and Peninsular Malaysia*. Kuala Lumpur: Oxford University Press.
Fraser, Nancy (1992) 'Rethinking the Public Sphere — A Contribution to the Critique

of Actually Existing Democracy' in C. Calhoun (ed.) *Habermas and the Public Sphere.* Cambridge, MA: MIT Press.

Gamson, William (1990) *The Strategy of Social Protest.* Belmont, California: Wadsworth Publishing Company.

Gitlin, Todd (1998) 'Public spheres or public sphericules', in T. Liebes and J. Curran (eds.) *Media, Ritual and Identity.* London and New York: Routledge.

Gitlin, Todd (1980) *The Whole World is Watching.* Berkeley: University of California Press.

Giroux, Henry (1998) 'Teenage Sexuality, Body Politics, and the Pedagogy of Display' in Jonathan Epstein (ed.) *Youth Culture: Identity in a Postmodern World.* Malden, MA and Oxford: Blackwell Publishers.

Goffman, Erving (1969) *Strategic Interaction.* Philadelphia: University of Pennsylvania Press.

Goffman, Erving (1959) *The Presentation of Self in Everyday Life.* Garden City, NJ: Doubleday.

Goldfarb, Jeffrey (1998) *Civility and Subversion: The Intellectual in Democratic Society.* Cambridge: University of Cambridge Press.

Griesman, H. C. (1977) 'Social Meanings of Terrorism, *Contemporary Crises.* 1: 307.

Gurvitch, Georges (1941) 'Mass, Community, Communion', *Journal of Philosophy.* 38.

Gusfield, Joseph R. (1995) 'Reflexivity of Social Movements' in Enrique Larana et. al. (eds.) *New Social Movements: From Ideology to Identity.* Philadelphia: Temple University Press.

Habermas, Jürgen (1989) *The Structural Transformation of the Public Sphere: An Inquiry into a Category of Bourgeois Society.* Cambridge, MA: MIT Press.

Hall, Stuart (1982) 'The Rediscovery of 'Ideology': Return of the Repressed in Media Studies' in G. Gurvevitch, et. al. (eds.) *Culture, Society and the Media.* London: Methuen.

Halton, Eugene (1995) *Bereft of Reason: On the Decline of Social Thought and Prospects for its Renewal.* Chicago and London: University of Chicago Press.

Handelman, Don (1990) *Models and Mirrors. Towards an Anthology of Public Events.* Cambridge: Cambridge University Press.

Hebdige, Dick (1989) 'After the Masses' in S. Hall and M. Jacques (eds.) *New Times: The Changing Face of Politics in the 1990s,* London: Lawrence and Wishart.

Heradstveit, Daniel and Bjørgo, Tore (1992) *Politisk kommunikation.* Lund: Studentlitteratur.

Hetherington, Kevin (1998) *Expressions of Identity: Space, Performance, Politics.* London: Sage.

Hetherington, Kevin (1994) 'The contemporary significance of Schmalenbach's concept of the Bund', *Sociological Review,* 42:1.

Hobsbawn, Eric (1959) *Social Bandits and Primitive Rebels.* Glencoe: University of Illinois Press.

Jakobson, Roman (1971) 'Two Aspects of Language and Two Types of Aphasic Disturbances", in R. Jacobson and J. Halle (eds.) *Fundamentals of Language* (Part II) Hague: Mouton.

Jenkins, Craig and Klandermas, Bert (eds.) (1995) *The Politics of Social Protest.* Minneapolis: University of Minneasota Press.

Kahane, Reuven (1997) *The Origins of Postmodern Youth.* Berlin and New York: Walter de Gruyter.

Kaplan, Carl (1999) 'For Their Civil Disobedience, the 'Sit-In' is Virtual'. *Cyber Law Journal.* kaplan@nytimes.com.
Keane, John (1991) *The Media and Democracy.* Cambridge, UK: Polity Press.
Keck, Margaret and Sikkink, Kathryn (1998) *Activists Beyond Borders: Advocacy Networks in International Politics.* Ithaca, N.Y.: Cornell University Press.
Kellner, Douglas (1995) 'Intellectuals and New Technologies', *Media, Culture & Society,* 17: 3.
Kertzer, David (1988) *Ritual, Politics, and Power.* New Haven and London: Yale University Press.
Kornhauser, A. (1959) *The Politics of Mass Society.* Glencoe, Ill.: Free Press.
Kosselleck, Richard (1988) *Critique and Crisis: Enlightenment and the Pathogenesis of Modern Society.* Oxford: Berg.
Lacqueur, Walter (1977) *Terrorism.* London: Weidenfeld & Nicolson.
Landzelius, Kyra (1998) 'Hunger Strikes: The Dramaturgy of Starvation Politics' in D. Aerts (ed.) *Einstein Meets Magritte: Science, Nature, Human Action & Society. Volume VIII: Man and Nature.* Dordrecht and New York: Kluwer Academic Publishers.
Le Bon, Gustave (1912) *Massans psykologi.* Stockholm: Bonniers.
Lemos, Andre´(1996) "The Labyrinth of Minitel" in Rob Shields (ed.) *Cultures of Internet: Virtual Spaces, Real Histories, Living Bodies.* London, Thousand Oakes and New Delhli: Sage Publications.
Lindholm, Charles (1990) *Charisma.* Oxford: Basil Blackwell.
Lovink, Geert (1997) 'Strategies for Media Activism', paper presented at 'Red Code' at The Performance Space, Sydney, November 23, 1997.
Lowry, Robert (1972) 'Toward a sociology of secrecy and security systems', *Social Problems.* 19:4.
Lukes, Stephen (1975) 'Political Ritual and Social Integration', *Sociology.* 9:2.
Lundström, Anna (1995) '"Vi äger gatorna i kväll!" Om hyllandet av Karl XII i Stockholm den 30 november 1991' in B. Klein (ed.) *Gatan är vår! Ritualer på offentliga platser.* Stockholm: Carlssons.
Lyman, Stanford (1964) 'Chinese Secret Societies in the Occident: Notes and Suggestions for Research in the Sociology of Secrecy', *Canadian Review of Sociology and Antropology.* 2.
Lyon, David (1994) *The Electronic Eye: The Rise of Surveillance Society.* Cambridge: Polity Press.
Lööw, Heléne (1994) 'Racist Youth Culture in Sweden: Ideology, Mythology and Lifestyle' paper presented at the NYRIS conference in Stockholm, May, 1994.
MacKenzie, David (1996) *Violent Solutions: Revolutions, Nationalism, and Secret Societies in Europe to 1918.* Lanham, Maryland, New York and London: University Press of America, Inc.
Maffesoli, Michel (1995) *The Time of the Tribes.* London: TCS and Sage.
Maffesoli, Michel (1996a) *Ordinary Knowledge: An Introduction to Interpetative Sociology.* Cambridge: Polity Press.
Maffesoli, Michel (1996b) *The Contemplation of the World: Figures of Community Style.* Minneapolis: University of Minnesota Press.
Mannheim, Karl (1952) *Essays on the Sociology of Knowledge.* London: Routledge and Kegan Paul.
Manning, Frank (1983) 'Cosmos and Chaos: Celebration in the Modern World' in F.

Manning (ed.) *The Celebration of Society*. Bowling Green, Ohio: Bowling Green University Popular Press.

Manning, P. K. (1996) 'Dramaturgy, Politics and the Axial Media Event', *The Sociological Quarterly*, 37:2.

Marx, Gary T. (1986) 'The Iron Fist in the Velvet Glove: Totalitarian Potentials Within Democratic Structures' in J. F. Short (ed), *The Social Fabric*. Beverly Hills, CA: Sage.

Massey, Doreen (1998) 'The Spatial Construction of Youth Cultures' in T. Skelton and G. Valentine (eds.) *Cool Places: Geographies of Youth Cultures*. London and New York: Routledge.

McCarthy, John and Wolfson, Mark (1992) 'Consensus Movements, Conflict Movements, and the Cooptation of Civic and State Infrastructures' in A. Morris and C. Mueller (eds.) *Frontiers in Social Movement Theory*. New Haven: Yale University Press.

McNair, Brian (1995) *An Introduction to Political Communication*. London and New York: Routledge.

McPhail, Clark and Wohlstein, Ronald (1986) 'Collective Locomotion as Collective Behavior', *American Sociological Review*. 51.

Melucci, Alberto (1995) *Challenging Codes: Collective Action in the Information Age*. Cambridge and New York: Cambridge University Press.

Melucci, Alberto (1989) *Nomads of the Present*. London: Hutchinson Radius.

Menand, L. and Schwartz, S. (1982) 'T. S. Eliot on Durkheim: A New Attribution', *Modern Philology*. 79.

Mestrovic, Stjepan (1991) *The Coming Fin de Siécle*. London: Routledge.

Moore, W. C. and Tumin, M. M. (1949) 'Some functions of ignorance', *American Sociological Review*. 14.

Nedelmann, Birgitta and Unguru, Sabetai (1998) 'Extreme Violence and Symbolic Meaning: The Case of the Suicide Bombers', *European Journal of Social Theory*. 4.

Negrine, Ralph (1996) *The Communication of Politics*. London: Sage.

Oberschall, Anthony (1978) 'The Decline of the 1960s Social Movements' in L. Kriesberg (ed.) *Research in Social Movements: Conflict and Change*. Vol. I. New Brunswick: JAI Press.

Park, Robert E. and Burgess, E. W. (1924) *Introduction to the Science of Sociology*. Chicago: University of Chicago Press.

Peirce, C. S. (1992) *The Essential Peirce: Selected Philosophical Writings*. N. Hauser and C. Kloesel (eds.) Bloomington, IN: Indiana University Press.

Peterson, Abby (1998) 'Durkheim og det 'magiske øyeblikket' ('Durkheim and the Magical Moment'), *Sosiologi i dag*. 28:1.

Peterson, Abby (1997a) *Neo-Sectarianism and Rainbow Coalitions: Youth and the Drama of Immigration in Contemporary Sweden*. Aldershot and Sydney: Avebury Press.

Peterson, Abby (1997b) 'Virtual Communities and Virtual Sects in the Post-Gutenburg Galaxy of Internet', *Tidskrift för Kultur Studier*. (3).

Peterson, Abby (1996a) 'Stranger or Guest?' in S. Fridlizius and A. Peterson (eds.) *Stranger or Guest? Racism and Nationalism in Contemporary Europe*. Stockholm: Almqvist & Wiksell International.

Peterson, Abby (1996b) review of Stepjan Mestrovic, *The Coming Fin de Siécle* and *The Barbarian Temperment* in *Acta Sociologica*. 39:4.

Peterson, Abby (1995) 'Walls and Bridges: Youth and the Drama of Immigration in Sweden', *Young*, (4).

Peterson, Abby (1994) 'Postmoderna pessimister', *Ord & Bild*, (3).
Peterson Abby (1992) *Women as Collective Actors - A Case Study of the Swedish Women's Peace Movement, 1898 - 1990*. Research report from the Department of Sociology, University of Gothenburg, no. 107.
Peterson, Abby (1989) 'Social Movement Theory', *Acta Sociologica*. 32:4.
Peterson, Abby and Thörn, Håkan (2000) 'Movimientos sociales y modernidad de los medios de comunicatioíon Industrias se los medios de comunication, amigos o enemigos?' *Comunicacion y Sociedad*. 35.
Peterson, Abby and Thörn, Håkan (1994) 'Social Movements as Communicative Praxis: A Case Study of the Plowshares Movement', *Young* 2: 2.
Pile, Steve (1997) 'Introduction: Opposition, political identites and spaces of resistance' in S. Pile and M. Keith (eds.) *Geographies of Resistance*. London and New York: Routledge.
Piven, Frances Fox and Cloward, Richard (1992) 'Normalizing Collective Protest' in A. Morris and C. Mueller (eds.) *Frontiers in Social Movement Theory*. New Haven: Yale University Press.
Quarterman, James (1993) 'The Global Matrix of Minds' in L. M. Harasim (ed.) *Global Networks* . Cambridge: MIT Press.
Rawls, Anne (1996) 'Durkheim's Epistemology: The Neglected Argument', *American Journal of Sociology*. 102:2.
Ricoeur, Paul (1981) *Hermeneutics and the Human Sciences: Essays on language, action and interpretation*. Cambridge: Cambridge University Press.
Robbins, Timm (1988) *Cults, Converts and Charisma: The Sociology of New Religious Movements*. London: Sage.
Roberts, John M. (1972) *The Mythology of the Secret Societies*. London: Secker & Warburg.
Robinson, JoAnn (1981) *Abraham Went Out: A Biography of A. J. Muste*. Philadelphia: Temple University Press.
Rochberg-Halton, Eugene (1982) 'Situation, Structure, and the Context of Meaning', *Sociological Quarterly*, 23.
Ruddick, Susan (1998) 'Modernism and Resistance: How 'Homeless' Youth Sub-Cultures Make a Difference' in T. Skelton and G. Valentine (eds.) *Cool Places: Geographies of Youth Cultures*. London and New York: Routledge.
Salomon, Kim (1996) *Rebeller i takt med tiden: FNL-rörelsen och 60-talets politiska ritualer*. Stockholm: Rabén Prisma.
Sartre, Jean-Paul (1976) *Critique of Dialectical Reason*. Jonathan Rée (ed.) London: New Left Reviews.
Schlesinger, Philip (1991) *Media, State and Nation*. London: Sage.
Schofer, Peter and Rice, David (1977) 'Metaphor, Metonymy, and Synecdoche Revis(it)ed', *Semiotica*. 21:1/2.
Schmalenbach, Herman (1977) 'Communion - A Sociological Category', in G. Lüschen and G. Stone (eds.), *Herman Schmalenbach: On Society and Experience*. Chicago: University of Chicago Press.
Schmid, Alex and de Graaf, Janny (1982) *Violence as Communication: Insurgent Terrorism and the Western News Media*. London: Sage.
Seel, Ben (1996) 'Frontline Eco-Wars! The Pollak Free State Road Protest Community: Counter-Hegemonic Intention, Pluralist Effects'. in Colin Barker and Mike Tydesley (eds.) *Alternative Futures and Popular Protest*. Manchester: The Manchester Metropolitan University.

Sennett, Richard (1976) *The Fall of Public Man: On the Social Psychology of Capitalism.* New York: Vintage Books.

Shils, Edward (1957) 'Primordial, Personal, Sacred and Civil Ties', *British Journal of Sociology.* 8: 2.

Shils, Edward (1956) *The Torment of Secrecy.* New York: Free Press.

Simmel, Georg (1950) *The Sociology of Georg Simmel.* (translated and edited by Kurt H. Wolff) Glencoe, Illinois: The Free Press.

Smelser, Neil (1962) *Theory of Collective Behaviour.* New York: Free Press.

Snow, David et al. (1986) 'Frame Alignment Processes, Micromobilization, and Movement Participation'. *American Sociological Review.* 51.

Snow, David and Benford, Robert (1988) 'Ideology, Frame Resonance, and Participant Mobilization' in *From Structure to Action: Comparing Social Movement Research Across Cultures,* Bert klandermans, Hanspeter Kriesi, and Sidney Tarrow (eds.). Vol. 1 of *International Social Movement Research.* Greenwich, Conn.: JAI Press.

Soja, E. (1989*) Postmodern Geographies: The reassertion of space in critical social theory.* London: Verso.

Szerszynski, Bronislaw (1996) 'Green Action, Green Virtue: Membership and Moral Experience in Radical Environmental Movements" in C. Barker and M. Tydesley (eds.) *Alternative Futures and Popular Protest.* Manchester: The Manchester Metropolitan University.

Tarrow, Sidney (1994) *Power in Movement: Social Movements, Collective Action and Politics.* Cambridge: Cambridge University Press.

Tarrow, Sidney (1989) *Democracy and Disorder: Protest and Politics in Italy 1965-1975.* Oxford: Oxford University Press.

Taylor, Verta and Whittier, Nancy (1992) 'Collective Identity in Social Movement Communities: Lesbian Feminism Mobilization' in A. Morris and C. Mueller (eds.) *Frontiers in Social Movement Theory.* New Haven: Yale University Press.

Taylor, Verta and Rupp, Leila (1993) 'Women's Culture and Lesbian Feminism Activism: A Reconsideration of Cultural Feminism', *Signs.* 19.

Thompson, John B. (1995) *Media and Modernity: A Social Theory of the Media.* Stanford, California: Stanford University Press.

Thörn, Håkan ((1999) 'Nya sociala rörelser och politikens globalisering: Demokrati utanför parlamentet?' in E. Amnå (ed.) *Civilsamhället.* Stockholm: Demokratiutredningen.

Thörn, Håkan ((1997) *Rörelser i det moderna: Politik, modernitet och kollektiv identitet i Europa 1789-1989,* Stockholm: Rabén & Prisma.

Thrasher, Frederic (1927 and 1960) *Gangs.* Chicago: University of Chicago Press.

Troeltsch, Ernst (1931) *The Social Teachings of the Christian Churches.* London: Allen and Unwin.

Turner, Bryan S. (1996) *The Body and Society.* London: Sage.

Turner, Victor (1969) The Ritual Process: Structure and Antistructure. Chicago: Adeline.

Virilio, Paul (1977) *Speed and Politics: An Essay on Dromology.* New York: Semiotext(e).

Wagner-Pacifici, Robin (1986*) The Moro Morality Play: Terrorism as Social Drama.* Chicago and London: University of Chicago Press.

Wark, McKenzie (1997) *Virtual Geographies.* Bloomington: University of Indiana Press.

Wirth, Louis (1964) *On Cities and Social Life. Selected Papers.* Chicago: Chicago University Press.

Wray, Stefan (1998a) 'Paris Salon or Boston Tea Party? Recasting Electronic Democracy, A View from Amsterdam.' Paper prepared for presentation at the seminar, 'Communication, Community and Democracy', Amsterdam, July 12-18, 1998.
Wray, Stefan (1998b) 'Rhizomes, Nomads, and Resistant Internet Us'. http://www.nyu.edu/projects/wray/RhizNom.html
Zald, Mayer and Useem, Bert (1987) 'Movement and Countermovement Interaction: Mobilization, Tactics and State Involvement', in M. Zald and J. McCarthy (eds.) *Social Movements in Organizational Society.* Cambridge, MA: Winthrop.